August Kibler's
Stories for Tyler
Voices of Context from Eden to Patmos

ISBN 978-1-7352332-3-9

www.straydog.press
info@straydog.press

Dedicated to Aurie Mitchell West
for the gifts of grace and friendship
she has generously given to us.

Book One: Voices of the Ancient

Book Two: Voices and the Peaceable One

An Afterword

Book One: Voices of the Ancient

The First Scapegoat

You might not think of me as
the first scapegoat in the
    patriarchal system,
but I ask that you walk for
a bit with me in the garden, as it were,
to see what might be there.

If you don't understand my life
    as a metaphor,
then I suggest you are very
likely to miss the whole point
    of this story.

    You make my life rather small and
pathetic when you try to make literal
my coming from the man's side,
my vulnerability to the serpent,
my own eating of the forbidden fruit,
my persuading of the man to eat.
    Small, because of the great
narrative of a blessed Creation, and pathetic,
because I am somehow the epitome
    of original sin.

What I and the man, the writer would
call Adam, are in the writer's mind is
the human's conscious awareness of the
    existence of evil. This was the fruit of
which we ate. You might think of it as
inevitable, which I suppose it was.
But, in the billions of years in which the
cosmos formed and the Creators

breathed life on
this small orb, the innocence was as
real as it is for any newborn child. Our ancestors
were not dumb. They were largely physically
and symbolically naked and unashamed.
        Creation was very good.

The "fall of man" was one poor species
        getting out of synch
with the Creators who loved all into being.
To my thinking, the writer could have
arrived at this point of the story without
        singling me out quite as he did.

Male and female were created in all species
of Creation. We didn't see the Creator
making the female fish from the male or
any other creature under heaven.
        Male and female we were created.
The writer must have been married, and his wife
must have nagged one too many times
about writing and not doing any needed
work around the place when
        he set the text to the scroll.
I can't say. I wasn't there. But it certainly
would explain a lot. That or perhaps
he was just one in a long line of chauvinistic
writers too insecure to look more
        honestly at themselves.

        The imagery of us coming from the
dust is a powerful one. We are as a
substance, one with all that is. I take no
exception there.

For all the flaws in telling and all the flaws
in how my story endures, my strongest

objection is being the first scapegoat.
The woman made me do it.
Really? This is higher consciousness?
The original blessing, which is certainly
the truth of our origin as a species,
becomes the original sin,
with me as the original scapegoat?
Our image with the Creators
gathering us under their wings to
open those wings and send us forth
on Creation's dawn
forever made small by the concept of
sin and shame devoid of this great
image of love? Our Mother Hen
protecting and nurturing her brood?

Yes, as a species, we forsake a more
innocent way for our own meddling
in a dualistic system of scapegoating
that, on its best day, is quite pitiful,
and on its worst
is absolute horror.
If my life as a metaphor
(or a literal meaning, if you must) is to
have any lasting value for humankind,
it is to return to the Garden
and walk again in its dawn when
all was blessed and good.
To find myself, yourself, once again
naked and unashamed.
To be the Creators' beloved children
and no one's scapegoat.

The Old Man

You might think that we pre-flood folk lived
some mighty long lives. It is said I lived
    for nine-hundred sixty-nine years.
That was nothing compared to the ten
great men of Babylon who lived for over
    forty thousand years!
We rather pale in comparison. It isn't
only the old wives who have tales.
    I am what is considered a
pre-historic character, so attaching
too much around these stories of my
age is wasted effort.
    I would like to talk about
generational influences that you
might find useful. I can cover what
I need to in four generations—
    from my dad to my grandson.
It is a story of Grace and how easily it can be
    squandered for the violent way.

    My father, Enoch, was a man who
sought to walk among the divine presence.
I remember him as certainly not perfect,
but someone who sought to instill a humility
within me. He was kind and generous.
    I am not sure what became of Dad.
He was with us one day and nowhere to be
found the next. He was quite old. We surmised
he had either taken a long stroll with the
    Divine Presence and just kept on going,
or, like an old dog, wandered off to die in peace.
    These are perhaps the same thing.
There is much to be said for dying without
    many busybodies buzzing around,
trying to keep one alive when death has already

knocked on the door
or thinking they are somehow comforting.
　　Their fear of death
is little comfort and much annoyance.

　　I am wandering off-subject here a bit.
Suffice it to say, he had a good, full life and
was long-revered as a great ancestor.

　　I tried to be the kind of man
he would have respected. As best I could
tell, I was living up to his standards
pretty well. That is, until a
　　close look was taken at my son, Lamech.
If my grandfather had a grave, surely,
　　he rolled over in it.
We all struggled to understand honor,
shame, pride, retribution, vengeance,
and how all these relate to pleasing
　　or appeasing the Divine Presence.
Many believed the best one can do is
to appease. We sought to please.
　　Lamech stood out from the
rest. It seemed to me that he sought neither to
appease or please. He had a very
　　perverted sense of justice
and saw himself, not the Divine, as
　　the Great Avenger.

"I have killed a man for wounding me,
　　a young man for striking me.
If Cain is avenged sevenfold,
　　truly Lamech seventy-sevenfold."

That is a lot of rage-full revenge that
　　is, not surprisingly, very unfruitful.
He was both braggart and bully.

I did not approve, though I was unable
to assuage his temperament. It did
        nothing for the community at large,
which was sinking quickly into great
cycles of violence. It is hard to say that
he was indeed not the ringleader
        when practicing such injustice.

Noah found the Grace that Enoch and
I had known. This son of Lamech
        would try yet again to
walk humbly and serve. Grace is
a divine gift, but one that must be
claimed generation after generation.
        No one can claim it for another.
No inheritance can ensure a
        generation's walk in such Grace.
Noah understood this as his grand-
        father had understood it.
As I had understood it as well.

It is my prayer that somewhere in this
        family line,
not only will we find the Grace of
        my dad and grandson,
but One shall come one day from out of
our root and proclaim divine Grace for all.
That vengeance, in its contempt for mercy
and justice, will be seen for the cycle
of failure and misery it ensures.
That forgiveness and mercy shall be the way,
        not by happenstance, not as a one-off,
        but seventy-sevenfold.
An old man can dream, can't he?

The Woman of the Ark

Our story is common enough,
even if it may seem a bit extraordinary.
The oral tradition of our people and
of other lands share, amidst formidable
disasters, heroic tales of survival.
When a great flood
or another calamity comes, it is hard
to cope with loss and can be just as
hard to understand why a few
survive when many die.
We were the few who survived
this cataclysmic event.
The great rivers flooded
the world as we knew it,
taking with it hordes of city folk
and animals, wild and tame.
We tried to make sense of it, and
here is a bit of our story.

We were country folk. That is
important to know if you are to
understand our story. We lived
closely to the land and knew the
powers of small streams and great
rivers turning into torrents of
raging destruction.
The people of the cities and even
most small towns don't live with
this intimate connection, and
what we do in preparation
looks peculiar to them.
My husband had an acute sense
of stewardship and cared deeply
for the preservation of everything
around him.

7

People would think him a fool for
preparing for disasters, and never
more so than having a large ark
	ready and waiting for
the superstorm of the century
	(or perhaps, many centuries).

	He labored on the ark long enough
that it did begin to look a little
	over the top.
(He was willing to share his blueprints
with anyone interested. No one was.)

In reality, he planned for it to sustain us
for a lengthy time through the rain and
flood waters, along with all the different
	animals we could round up.
Neither of us would have been
sorry if it had never been needed,
	but the rains came down,
and the floods came up.
And we were safely onboard and
sealed in from the sudden inland sea.

Emerging afterward was difficult.
The destruction was total. What
we had known as villages and towns
were wiped out. Noah believed
	Yahweh had spared us
because of our obedience. He was a
good man and sought to listen to the
breathed Word of the Creators.
	I struggled with the devastation
around me. Standing in the light
with rains off in the distance often
produced the wonder of the rainbow.
It is hard to look at that and not

find ourselves hopeful.
Beauty brings hope. Seeing the
rainbow after the storm brought
us all hope. Hope that such would
    never again befall
us or another.   In reality, the
cycle of natural disasters continue
and shall continue, or so it would seem.
    Though, for our part,
we would never again see a flood
    such as this.
How are we to understand?

    We were not there when the
foundations were laid for the natural
laws. Still, there is more to be grateful
for than we can often comprehend.
The free gifts of Creation were renewed
again and again, from the high peaks
of the ever-changing mountains to the
    deepest depths of the sea.
The sprouting shoots and blooming
flowers. The honey bees back to their
    diligent labors, sharing their
sweet purity. The gentle shower
that softens the land around us. The
flashes of lightning that amaze. Birds
and deer and sheep who, like us, are
bringing to life the next generation
    in all their fragility.
That amazing rainbow offering hope.
    All signs of the Creators'
loving into being we, who struggle to
    love and to understand.

Call Me Ishmael

I hardly know where to begin.
Yes, my father was Abram,
     my mother, his slave.
While technically my mother served as
the woman of the house, on the books,
     she belonged to my father.
As did numerous concubines. After
the woman of the house was dead, he
would take another wife, Keturah.
She would bear six more sons. I would be
gone by then.

     I doubt I was the oldest
of his offspring. I was the first
to be openly acknowledged,
     which the woman of the house
would raise holy-hell about more
than once—ultimately leading to
me being put out in the desert.
     There were many young
girls and boys running around the
encampment, all with familial
     resemblance to my father.
     Many older than me.
None of the daughters were ever
acknowledged. I guess father didn't
get the memo on equality
at Creation. There were strict
rules around inheritance, and
     we men had the edge. I had
the leading edge for a time, as
the oldest. The woman of the house
would see to it that never happened.

It is important for context to know

that we did not possess scrolls filled
    with laws and doctrines.
Creation was our instructor. Most
peoples believed in various gods
for various things. Having observed
    nature's violent moments
and unpredictable rains, it became
common custom to make sacrifices
to these many gods in hopes of
    appeasement and good fortune.
Our father had only a slightly
different view, which was rather than
having to appease many gods, there
was one god who had breathed us into
being and thus one god who we were
    to worship.
Appeasement often called for ritual
sacrifice to be sure god or the gods
    was or were cognizant of the clan's devotion.
They weren't above human sacrifice,
and bird, lamb, and calf might be burned
as well. The gods liked blood and fire,
    as best we could tell.
Decisions on what and when to sacrifice
was made by the lead male of the group.
    (Women had no say in such matters.)

I'm not sure how we boys got so
consumed with our dominance in
    the economic and moral order.
We had an oral tradition, which suggested
the woman came from our rib and
it was that same woman who first offended the
gods. The proof of this offense was
    women's labor pains.
Only vengeful gods would impart this
kind of pain for such an elemental

act as giving birth.
    Of course, we also observed male
dominance in the animal order.
    Any herdsman and hunter
knows enough of nature to see that the
ram may breed with many ewes, battling other
rams for supremacy. Ultimately,
the old ram is too weak to dominate,
    and another takes his place.
(We tended to dismiss the ewes' management
of the herd and their nurturing of those
young, weak rams-to-be.)

And if there were monogamous species
out there, we weren't about to go looking
    to them as examples.

As with any power structure, inertia
has its effect. By my time in history,
we men had control locked up tightly.
It was not unique to our clan.
The patriarchal model was firmly
    ingrained across clans.
Enough on that. You get the point.

There were intermittent exceptions
to this rule, and nowhere more so
    than in the clan of Abram.
Father caved into the woman
of the house, whether a good idea
or not. It seemed to many of us that
    not good was the norm.

I could have really grown bitter.
    And, like Cain,
I might well have murdered my
    half-brother, Isaac.

Even in premeditated cold blood.
Ours was a different history from
      Cain and Abel.
Isaac and I got along fine. I enjoyed
having a younger brother.
(One of Isaac's sons would one day
marry one of my daughters.)

Unlike the woman of the house towards me,
my mother was nurturing and kind to
Isaac. Our father genuinely loved us both.
      My mother was used and abused.
There is no skirting around this.
The woman of the house did wrong
by her on so many occasions it was
hard to keep track. When the
      long years of bitterness of not
having her own child ended,
the worst was yet to come. She became
obsessed with making sure her
own son inherited everything and
in turn impressed on father the
narrative that their legacy would
      only continue through Isaac.
She wanted my mother and me put away.
The one god was invoked as needed
      to confirm father and the woman's decisions.

Her obsession led to my expulsion.
I'm sure she would have been all
too pleased had I gone off and died in
the desert. I was more loved than that.
      I would survive
and actually thrive. Isaac and I would
both have great familial legacies.
As we drifted apart and generation
led to generation, our language and

dialect would drift apart as well.
       As our father had taught
us both, we looked to the one God.
The clan of Isaac would call this
       one god Yahweh.
My decedents, Allah. That such should
       ever have been seen as division
is a failure neither Isaac nor I could
have ever foreseen. I suppose it
       is a bad fruit of a chosen-ness
inherent in our family's story
that overlooked the shared dignity
       of us all.
You have to ask, what is in a name
when faith abides in the great Creators?
       I can't answer that.
I don't believe it can be answered
       except perhaps as this:
making the god in their own image.
       Small and petty as they.
The many gods of other clans seem
       less idolatrous than this.

The Ghosts of Sodom

We are haunted by our legacy.
The evil of our day was, in ignorance,
    cast upon others in a net of
deception that was not of our making.

The poets understood our evil.
For some reason, the clergy and
lawmakers would not. We are
not suggesting the destruction
    that befell us was unjust.
Quite to the contrary, the evil
we had succumbed to recoiled upon us.
    One could not say
    it was not just.

We had fallen into the deepest
cesspool of inhumanity. We
    broke the essential goodness
of the Creators. We not only
did not care for the poor, the
orphan, and the stranger, but we were
consumed! Robbing, raping,
    murdering, and
    exploiting anyone we could.

(For the record, others have done as much
and escaped our more immediate fate.)

We had failed to be a neighbor
    even to ourselves.
Our community—wholly corrupted.

To hear the voices of later centuries,
you would think we were some
    gay ghetto with

15

gay bars and gay pride parades.
Sorry to disappoint you, but you
    got that all wrong.
We failed to love. We did so
so completely!

Oh, we had glitter and bling! We
had all the glitz any city could
market to attract consumers.
    But this is quite irrelevant
to our story.

We sought no relief while we lived.
Our contempt for forgiveness
    was as vehement as our lust
for the intoxicating temptations
we clawed and grabbed for.
    From our haunted graves,
we rise again, seeking the welfare
of the generations who followed us.
    Know love. Know peace.
We knew neither love nor peace.
    We died as we had lived.
Consumed. Had we honored
the free gifts of Creation, we would
have discovered grace upon grace.
    We created hell.
Others, too, would find it by
    their own choice.
The testament of our destruction
has done little to instruct the
    lust and greed and exploitation
of those after us. Sadly,
    our sin endures.

Young Ben

I was the youngest of the family.
My mother, Rachael, would die
as she gave me life. As she lay dying,
she named me Ben Oni,
    "son of my mourning."
My father, an old man, didn't
want to attach grief to me. He called
me Ben Yamin, "son of my days."
    Just call me Ben for short.
I like Ben. It honors them both.

What can I tell you about life with
    eleven older brothers?
Not all were Rachael's sons. Most
were sons of my Aunt Leah.

(Step-mother if you prefer. Modern
families can be quite confusing!)

    The one brother I shared
as a child of Jacob and Rachael
    was Joseph.
To say Joseph thought of himself
as special would be an understatement.
    Father and Mother did spoil him.
I may have been the youngest, but
    Joseph was the baby.
Leah was not his first choice in marriage.
Our granddad was a conniver
    and tricked my father into
the marriage. After more years of labor,
he could finally marry his true love.
    And so, it was Joseph who was
the first fruit of that love. It might
have been better for all of us if

Granddad hadn't interfered
with love in the first place.

The other brothers were tired
of Joseph lording his specialness over
them. The truth of their remedy
would remain unknown to me
        and my father for many years.
The brothers said he had been
        killed by a wild beast,
and so mother and father grieved his death.
(I am told my mother's wailing seemed endless.)
The joy was now mostly gone from father.
        He also became more protective
of me, as you might well imagine.

After several years had passed,
        times got very hard.
There had been severe drought
that extended from one season
to another to another. Our
livestock couldn't eat dirt,
        and neither could we.
Our grains failed. Our herds began
to die out. We were desperate but
not bankrupt. Father had kept
money aside for these cycles of despair.
        Thanks to his good
stewardship, we were as well-off
as any could have been under the
circumstances. And so, my brothers
set off for Egypt where we heard
        there was food for sale.

Of this it must be said of my
        brother Joseph,
when it came to conniving,

Granddad had nothing on him.
    You might say he came by it
honestly, but he possessed it in spades.
    Of course, he had not died.
    My other brothers had sold
him off as a slave. From there,
Yahweh only knows, how exactly
    he was able to connive
his way not only to freedom but
to gain favor with Pharaoh himself.
He had his story. I had my doubts
    on some of the details.

    As Chief Operations Officer
in great favor with Pharaoh,
he managed the expansion of a
seven-year grain purchasing program,
    buying grain at below-market
prices during productive years and
storing it in a large complex
of storage barns he had had local slaves
build just for this program.
    As families like ours became
desperate, he would slowly turn the
    crank of the empire on them.
At first, taking what money they had.
    Then, any remaining livestock
and goods. And when all this was gone,
their land itself and their freedom
    were the price for life.
The land and the people were
    Pharaoh's possession.

When my other brothers arrived into this
scheme, Joseph recognized them and
began playing games with them. They
made mention of a younger brother

19

when he pressed them
on details of the family.
    He insisted they return
with me, which mystified us all.
My father feared losing his only
    other son with Rachael.
The stress on such an old man was
not good. And it would only get
worse when this Egyptian COO tried
to hold me over on false charges of theft.
    Judah begged the COO to
imprison him rather than me so
as to spare our father the
    sure and certain grief
that might well be the old man's demise.

    Thanks to Judah's pleading,
guilt finally overcame his crafty games,
and he broke down in tears and
    confessed his identity.
Of course, we were dumbfounded.

I'd like to say our family's
    reconciliation
ended happily ever after. Sure,
    we survived the famine.
Did Joseph ever get word to us
and others in the land that
the famine was coming, as he
asserted he had known and advised
    Pharaoh about? He did not.
We lost our family lands to the COO's
    foreclosure program—perhaps
not as overtly as others, but the
    end result was the same.

The old man was told to leave with all his

children, grandchildren, and hirelings
    and move to this foreign land.
The only way the COO would
    reunite the family,
supposedly for our long-term welfare.
    Our father pleaded with Joseph to
see to it he was buried in his homeland.
    This he granted.
    What I learned from all this?
Beware of older brothers!

    Our comfort and security
was short-lived. The screws
of the empire turned tightly on us.
    Our children and our
children's children would know only
    a life of slavery
    for the next
four hundred years.

The Sister of the Exodus

I am Miriam,
a daughter of the house of Levi.
Much of my life has been denied
basic freedom, as our clan and I
    were enslaved laborers
for the Pharaoh of Egypt. This was
    not a recent development but one
that dated back hundreds of years
when our ancestor Jacob was forced
here by his son, the COO of the
Egyptian Empire. That is a long
and complicated story that has already been
told. There is nothing I could add
to the telling of it.

There is an aspect
of our history that is important
to share. Levi was one of the
    twelve sons of Jacob,
and it was the twelve clans of
these sons who constituted the
enslaved laborers. The patriarch of
these clans was our ancestor Abraham.

Abraham passed onto to his own
clan his understanding that, unlike
most other peoples, including these
Egyptians who worshiped many gods,
    we were to worship one god.
During our captivity, we were
    faithful to his instruction.
The enslaver can rob us of our
dignity, but they cannot rob us of
    our faith and hope.
We held onto this knowledge tightly and

to the hope that the one god
would free us from our bondage.
    To my mind, that one god moved
very, very slowly. There was no sign
of impending freedom when I was a
    young girl, with women and children
stomping mud in the clay pits. It looked
like my descendants would be forced labor
    for many more generations.

Despite being captives against our
will, we grew and knew relative peace,
if not prosperity or comfort. We
    were worked very hard,
and things seemed only to get worse
    as our numbers grew.
Pharaoh wanted to cut our strength
lest we get our own ideas of rebellion,
even though we desired to live peaceably.
    He believed he had persuaded
the Egyptian midwives who served
our people to kill newborn boys.
    Persuading life-giving women
to kill wasn't his most successful
program. They reported back that,
because of our strength, the births
were done by the time they arrived.
    He then resorted to ordering his
minions to cull the empire of young
boys by throwing them into the Nile.
    Men like killing. This plan
held more promise for the desired end.

    My mother tried to hide her
newborn boy in the reeds along the Nile.
When Pharaoh's daughter found the
infant, she took him to be her own.

Of course, she needed a wet nurse,
and so it was that my mother was able to
serve the woman in the palace and
nurture her own son, whom the woman
     would name Moses.

He certainly grew up with a privileged
existence none of us can quite imagine.
Mother was able to foster some long-term
     ties with the boy because of her
relationship with the woman of the palace.
     He also grew up with the influence of
privilege the empire instilled and the
willingness to use violence as one of many
remedies. Perhaps Moses understood
this all too well. On seeing one of his
fellow Hebrews beaten by a task master
for the empire, Moses, thinking
he was unseen, struck down the man
and buried him. He had been seen, however,
     and had to flee the empire to
escape Pharaoh's judgment.

In his years away, he encountered
the spirit of the one god who refused
to be nailed down to the constraints
     of name and characteristics.
This god was "Being." This was all he
really knew. Moses returned with
     a new and profound liberation
manifesto. The seat of Pharaoh had
passed to the heir, and Moses and
my brother boldly went to this new ruler,
whom Moses had known as a boy,
     and demanded our freedom.
It was long, drawn out, and a time of great
mystery, fear, and hope.

Our day of freedom finally came.
In retrospect, it would have been better
    had we left with only the bare
necessities, but the reality is that we plundered
whatever we could get our hands on.
This was, I believe, our first real act of
idolatry against the one god of Being.
    It would not be the last.

Moses was somehow made of firmer stock
than either my brother Aaron or me. He
faithfully honored the one god of Being
while we, with the others, were glad
enough to build a golden calf. The
plundering had given us gold for
which there was little use but to worship.
    As I said, better if we'd
left what the Egyptians valued
and stuck to the gift of freedom we
    had finally secured.
At every turn, we found ourselves
extolling the safety of enslavement
over the freedom of our present day.
    Moses had to put up with a
lot, and whenever he disappeared
to listen to the one god of Being,
we would degenerate into a
    great society of complainers
and ignore any contemplation of the
    one god of Being.

    For my part, I was rather harsh on
who was in and who was out. My
mindset was contrary to Moses'. I
didn't want liberation theology. I wanted
rules and rituals. When Moses wanted
to marry the Ethiopian Cushite, Aaron

and I both objected. Aaron was a priest
and didn't approve. It didn't help
that I stirred him up about this.

    It is easy to affirm a priestly
mind of exclusion.

    The one god of Being, as usual,
seemed to align with Moses. I was
mysteriously inflicted with leprosy
all over my body. I was going to have
      to put bigotry aside
if I were to recover.

In many respects, Moses was a
true messenger of the one god
of our father Abraham. He ministered
through justice, truth, and reconciliation.
He led us from bondage to what
should have been a land flowing
      with milk and honey for all.
Sadly, most of our clan could not
trust such a benevolent and free society.

    That plunder, and the greed
and retribution that drove it, had
infected our hearts. We would only
trust gold as our god, armies as our
protectors, death and destruction
      as our liberators,
and myriad laws to judge, control,
and condemn.

The great liberation theology of
      Abraham, Jacob, and Moses
would be lost. What was known
as the great Covenant with the
      one god of Being,
which would ensure our goodwill if we
could but commit to righteousness,

justice, steadfast love,
mercy, and faithfulness, would be
mocked for all intents and purposes.
The laws and powers that were
to follow would serve these up on
our own terms as we saw fit.

We would do the unthinkable.
We would enslave ourselves.

The Priestly Instructions

During the days of Moses, we seized
the opportunity to expand on the
law of the stone tablets. People want
    specificity, and there can be
little argument that when it comes
to specificity, we excel! No one could
    offer specifics like we could.
Moses had grown a bit weary trying
to keep everyone in line. He gave us
    carte blanche
to draft and ratify the Mosaic Law to
ensure the security of our new state.
    It was a work in progress up to
and following his death. We just added
to the omnibus bill he had authorized,
which secured its legitimacy in law.

Law by committee can take on a life
of its own, and certainly, our body
    of lawmakers
was no exception. We drilled
more and more into the granular
    details of life. We included
rubrics for the clergy; instructions
on ordination; purity codes as they
applied to animals, diseases, and
menstrual cycles; rules for
purification and holiness codes
for sex, sacrifices, crimes, festivals, and
Sabbath-keeping; and finally, our
    catch-all for things abominable.
It seems safe to say we had things
    covered!

Of course, there was one major problem

once the work of the committee was
done and the scroll was added to
    the Torah.
A major problem, but we worked always
    to mitigate its real impact.
Only the dishonest could ever claim
to keep it. We in the temple
    peddled our holiness,
and the commoners generally
bought into the system. Not that
    they had any choice.
The laws we set forth were used to keep
order well enough — most of the time.
We did get some pushback from outsiders.
The complaint was always the same:
    its effectiveness
in honoring justice in the
    Covenant with Yahweh.

    The worst of the lot were
the poets coming along and
subverting the system. They suggested
Yahweh is merciful, and we were
strong advocates of the
    honor/shame culture.
You couldn't be wishy-washy and
    ready to forgive
in lieu of the prescribed punishments
we had put in place.
    As a consequence,
we were just as much at odds with
the poets as we were with the
    commoners and their
    rabble-rousers.
The law was ours to enforce,
    not theirs!
After all, we were its authors and

perfecters. Its judge and jury.

You will have guessed by the tenor
of the laws that our committee was
all male. As Eve had been the first to
sin, she had set the standard
for male control. We couldn't
    hope to have an orderly
community with weak women in
any seat of authority.
    Our harshest judgments
were against women who had lost their
virginity to anyone other than their
husband. If unmarried and raped,
the rapist was expected to marry the
woman and could never divorce her.
    This was for her own well-being,
as who would have her after that?
We were equally harsh with any
man or woman who had any kind
of physical deformity. Clearly,
    Yahweh had punished them.
They were not welcome to eat the
bread of the temple and defile
    it and us by their presence.
We didn't want to look at them,
    and the laws made that possible.

We had rules for men, too, lest you
    think we were total misogynists.
For example, no bastard son could ever
be ordained or hold any kind of
position of authority. After all,
his mother had clearly been defiled.
Men were also not to get intimate
with each other. Our social order had
    no place for two men in love.

We couldn't have people questioning
what was going on behind closed doors
    in our temple leadership.

There were always those who, in
    their overactive imaginations,
believed the law could be boiled
down to these simple commandments:
Love Yahweh, and love your
    neighbor as yourself.
That all sounds nice, but it is hardly
the reality in the administration of an
economy. Suggesting that this supersedes
the law is sheer naiveté.
    Their imaginings
never penetrated our ranks in any
real measure. Our priority was order
and security. Only law and order
    could maintain the system,
and we were tough on crime!

    In the end, touchy-feely poets
and rabble-rousers were powerless.
    We had the death
penalty to wield a broad swath of
    justice as we defined it.
Poets could protest all they wanted.
    Retribution and death prevailed,
as did our control.

Achan of the Tribe of Judah

Confession is good for the soul,
they say. It may be good for the soul,
     but it didn't do my body any good.
As best I could see, the rules of warfare
were pretty loose. Killing and pillaging
were the norm. When Joshua surmised
that I had taken a garment, silver, and
gold for my personal possessions, he
     begged me to confess.
I said exactly what I had done and where
they would find the items. I held
nothing back from my confession. For that,
     I—and the rest of household—were stoned.
     Yes, even the animals,
as though this would somehow purge
evil from Israel once and for all.
     Somehow, this honored Yahweh.

Joshua wasn't against the spoils of war
     so long as they
went to the temple. It seemed to me
that Yahweh's will looked an awful
lot like Joshua's will. And if Yahweh
was as vengeful to women, children,
and animals as the great warrior and his
troops, then one had to wonder why
     humankind was ever created in
the first place. Either Yahweh likes
misery in his children, or we weren't
getting it. My suspicion was the latter.
     To continually war and kill?
To forever purge evil offenders like
me as though killing will end evil?
     What I lacked in character
at least I made up for in honesty.

My mercenary conquests were barely
different from our national agenda.
    My sin was to circumvent
the powers that be. A sure way to have
those powers come crashing down
    upon me. Little did I realize
that the stones would crash down
on my children as well.
    Justice perverted.
He, the divinely endowed.
    Me, the villain.
My family, victims of my villainy
and his. As those stones came
hurling towards us, I finally
felt the full measure of the
    violence by which we
claimed divine right. Whatever
it was we were doing, there was
    nothing divine about it.
We were just on the winning side
for now. Yahweh have mercy on us
when we might again be on the losing side.
    I suspect that will be soon enough.
What goes around comes around.

Perhaps one day, our people will be
led by a new Joshua. One who
will speak to peace and forsake conquest.
    One who will look at me,
my children, and the men, women,
and children of every town and village
and suggest that if any stand without sin,
    let them
    cast the first stone.

Call Me Mara

Of living in hardship and grief,
    I am no stranger.
    I wish I were.

We were a small family and
very poor. We found ourselves
unable to cope in our hometown
any longer, as the famine was
    taking its toll.

We heard things were better in
Moab. The life of an immigrant
    is frightening.
    You are judged
on every level—on every difference
between you and the citizenry.
But we had each other, and so,
with my husband and two sons,
    we set out.

We found food. We would
almost begin to thrive a bit.
    My two sons fell in love
and were married. My husband
and I accepted their Moabite
wives as our own daughters. But our
happiness was not to last.
    My husband died.
He died not long after we
arrived in Moab, and my two
sons saw me through my grief
    and cared for me.

    Now, ten years after our
departure from Bethlehem, they both

were dead, leaving me and my
daughters-in-law at a loss.
There was no social safety net
for three women.
We had to consider what to do.

I urged them to return to their families.
You are still young.
Make a life for yourselves!
I, too, would go back to my people.

Both protested while knowing the
difficulty of our predicament. Finally,
Orpah was persuaded,
kissed me, and left.
Ruth would not go. There was no
dissuading her. She would keep
her vows to her husband throughout
my bitter existence. My people would
be hers. My God her God.

When we returned to Bethlehem,
my dead husband's young cousin was doing
quite well for himself. Ruth
gleaned in his fields to get us the
basic provision of daily bread.

My bitter days would end. This
cousin might have rejected the
immigrant woman.
The Moabite widow.
Instead, he was to fall in love with Ruth.
Her devotion to me ended
the bitter chain of grief
the two of us had endured.
My bitterness would turn to joy.

And Moabite blood would forever
mingle in the kinship of the
    House of Bethlehem
and the kings and carpenters who
would spring from the tree of
    Boaz and Ruth—
    the branch of Jesse.

The First and Last Wives of the King

   i. The First Wife
When it comes to understanding
   ingratitude, I am a master!
My marriage was a power brokerage
between my father, Saul, and that
blowhard everyone seemed to admire,
   David.

You may recall the bargain on which
I was procured. If David could bring
my father, the king, one hundred
Philistine foreskins, he could have
   my hand in marriage.
(Family values!)

To be clear, that was my father's
condition—not mine! I'm sure he
thought David would get killed
in the process, which would mean
   one less ego to contend with.

To my misfortune, David returned
with *two hundred* foreskins, and
   my fate was sealed
in the warring madness of men.

Having fallen into that blunder,
my father would trade me off
   to Paltiel as his wife
in an attempt to keep
David from the throne. Well,
at least this husband was a loving man.

David never once expressed any
   love for me.

He was happiest when he was
showing off in public, particularly
    when parading around
    half-naked.

He would collect wives as he
collected foreskins. Nineteen
sons and one daughter from a
    number of wives.

    The last wife
would connive to make her son
the king, despite the long line of
heirs ahead of him.

She would ultimately succeed, and he
would even outdo his father on
    collecting wives.
Fortunately, I would die
long before I had to see all this.

Don't romanticize my days with David.
    We spend too much of our history
trying to make heroes where there
are none. At best, my father and his
successor ruled through
    a glass darkly.
While maybe not the worst of history,
they're hardly heroes in my book.

At least Paltiel would love me.
    "Oh, Michal!"
He would weep mightily whenever David
grabbed me back as his
possession—David's direct line
to the royal lineage.

Neither king would ever ask
me what I might want. Both
were more concerned with
        conquest than with love.

        ii. The Last Wife
Men need a women to blame.
Be they powerful or not, why
own up when you can
        blame a woman?

        Honestly, all I was doing was
bathing, as was prescribed for
all women coming out of their
menstrual cycle. It's not like
we had indoor plumbing! When
we bathed, weather permitting,
        we bathed in the river
        or in our own back gardens.

Yes, I was beautiful. I was also
married to a good man. It was
the lustful king who saw me and
decided his desire was stronger
        than his moral fortitude.
A few from the Palace Guard
came to fetch me for his pleasure.

Romanticize it if you must, but
where is the romance? He
made me pregnant, killed my husband,
        and took me for his wife.

Nathan knew what he had done and
called him out on it. The king would
        show some remorse,
but he could hardly let me back into

the world now that I was carrying
　　his child.

The child would die, but others
would soon follow. My beauty
drew him. I decided the least I could
do was forge an alliance with Nathan,
　　who "knew where the bodies were buried,"
to undo his kingship and make our
　　second son the king.

It took many years, but at last, my
son Solomon was king. Sadly,
he would follow in his father's
footsteps when it came to
　　collecting wives.

"Anything David can do I can do
better" seemed to be his motto.
　　What's a mother to do? Pray!
Pray for women everywhere.
　　Pray for women of all time.

Maybe one day, a more humble
shoot will spring from this branch,
the house of David of Bethlehem.
　　That is my hope.
　　That is my prayer.
And may he never be a collector of wives.

The Poets of the Hymnal

Art, music, and poetry
all emote the basic, raw, and
generally unfiltered story of
    the human condition.
Over time, several of us contributed
to one particular scroll that was
used as our hymnody for singular
reflection and communal worship.
At least one writer didn't get the memo
    of "keep it short and to the point."
Making it through the litany of
reverence for statue and ordinance
may well be a good discipline for
the flock, but it could be tiresome
and tended to be a bit too close to
    legalism for most of us.
Some liked that sort of thing, and
    so it stood.

    The harp or lute was
our typical instrument, though in
our imagination, things did
occasionally bend towards
instrumental merriment.
    Cymbals, drums, pipes—
nothing could hold us back!
In these moments, the charism
of Yahweh was upon us, and
    our souls burst forth with joy!
This was more the exception
than the rule. Mostly, our poetry
and chants were simple statements
of our pastoral life at its most basic—
the peace that we derived when
    life was in balance

41

and we prayed for all we loved.

To be sure, life was not always in balance,
and when it wasn't, no cymbal,
drum, or pipe could drown
        out our bitter anguish
or our litany of grievances.
We didn't quit writing our poetry
in these times, nor did the community
        refrain from joining us
in mournful melancholic melodies,
setting these words to
        corporate song.
We were all in the funk together,
and when this happened, our
        requests to Yahweh
were as bitter as our mood. We
never shied away from the
abandonment we sometimes felt nor
the retribution we hoped would
        befall our oppressors
and our enemies. In these times,
        our thoughts showed no mercy.
We spared no one. No matter how
innocent, we called for their blood.
        For their children's heads to be
dashed against the rock.
We did admit these were dark and
difficult days. Yet, they were never
        days that lingered long.
In brighter times, we would ponder
whether these should come out
        of the scroll.
To do so would have made us look
better, perhaps, but the intellectual
honesty of our poetry would have
        been a mockery to Yahweh,

who knew our thoughts.
Yahweh shall not be mocked.
This much we trusted of our
    understanding of the Covenant.

And so, the darkness of the hours
stood beside the brilliance of the days.
We ensured, too, that the scroll
would not end on such a dark note
as to suggest that we would find ourselves
    hopeless.
Quite the opposite. We ended with
    great praise from every voice
and every instrument under heaven
    dancing wildly, joyfully, with
all the exuberance of the dawn of
Creation! Praise the Creator
    of all that is!
The bitterness can never prevail!
Crash the cymbal!
    Let us be glad!
Blow the trumpet! Let us be joyful!
    Babbling brook, roaring river,
mighty volcano, tympani roll,
trumpet blow, cymbals crash,
every creature singing and dancing!
    Praise the Love
of this incredible cosmos!
    Hallelujah!

The Ammonite Queen

When you are one among
    seven hundred wives
and some three hundred concubines,
you might think you would have an identity
complex. My husband collected
    wives for military and economic
alliances. I'm not sure where I fit
into his conquest exactly. We were
a fairly suspect clan, having been
    descendants of Lot and one
of his daughters in a rather irrational
act of procreation brought on, no doubt,
by the post-traumatic stress of barely
    escaping the destruction
of Sodom and Gomorrah in which the
    matriarch had perished.
Be that as it may, I was the first wife of Solomon,
mother of prince Rehoboam and thus
    Queen of the realm,
but powerless under the great king.

    Solomon came to the throne
through no small wrangling and was thus
paranoid early on about shoring up
    his power.
He killed anyone he perceived might
be an enemy. He wasn't particularly
careful about who made the list.
    From there, he quickly
moved to increase his influence
in the region. He was eager to build the
long-anticipated temple in Jerusalem.
His father and king, David, never got the job
done. It was strongly held that this job was
    Solomon's to do.

His devotion to the task was obvious,
    but his motivation was not
nearly so clear-cut. For, you see,
    he gladly built temples
for every wife of convenience from
all those many and varied alliances.
    We had gods on display
in every city, town, and village. If the
    Yahweh of my ancestors Abraham
and Lot and the offspring of Jesse
was supposed to be the one god of
the empire, then Solomon had failed.
    He had failed.
He sold out! There is hardly any other
way to spin it. The empire narrative
was to cover this up in great stories of
    his wisdom, divinely given.
His accumulated wealth from all
these alliances as proof of his
    blessing from Yahweh.

I can't think Yahweh was too pleased
with any of it. Sure, the king managed
    to unify the empire more than any had
before him, but it was, in many ways,
    little more than a shell game.
It was based on murdering enemies
and many financial favors. This never
makes for long-term sustainability.
And there are always many who are
envious and wanting more, as well as
    opposition
from those left out in the cold.
For all his so-called wisdom, Solomon had
no egalitarian sense of justice. The
    Covenant of Yahweh,
nothing more than temple recitation.

Something for the priests to
ritually recognize on High Holy Days.

The kingdom my son would inherit
was already coming apart at the seams.
        Rehoboam would never be
king of the united realm as Solomon
had been. How could he?
When one strong-arm leader is gone,
        alliances collapse quickly
        and often violently.
All that pent-up envy and rejection comes
pouring out from every nook and cranny.
All the consolidation of wealth in the
        palace created great resentment.
The temple had its own prostitution ring.
The idolatry and perversion that was
rampant at the time made it impossible to
        keep up appearances any longer.
It could finally be acknowledged that
        all was not well within the realm.
The iron rule of Solomon would not
go away because my son was now king.
As his father had started out, so my
son would attempt to do in even greater
measure. "For whereas my father
        put a heavy yoke upon you,
I will put more to your yoke:
my father chastised you with whips, but
        I will chastise you with scorpions."

        Oy vey!
To think our ancestors Abraham and Lot
        had advocated for mercy.
What have we become?

The Rebellious Poet

Not everyone endowed with gifts is
    open to using them.
I was under some pressure to preach,
as I supposedly had gifts in this area.
I am generally considered one of the poets.
    I was not convinced of this.

The Great Voice circled me for weeks,
breathing into me words that I
was to go to Nineveh and preach, as
    they had lost their way.
She had to have her wires crossed!
This was the capital city of another
empire. The Assyrians were anything
    but friendly to Israel.
What did a Hebrew like me
    have to do with them?
And if Yahweh wanted to save them
from their wickedness, I couldn't see
    why I was needed.
Surely Yahweh could have intervened
more directly with someone already
there and knowledgeable of the
    political realities.
We are talking about one of the
major cities of our day. Sure, I was
just going to march in there, hold
a tent revival, and turn everything
around. Even if gifted with the Word,
    I was no miracle worker!

I'd been pestered long enough.
    I was *not* going to Nineveh!
The best plan seemed to be to get far
away. I'd get my mind off all this by

going on a Mediterranean cruise.
What it would lack in accommodations
and amenities it would make up for in
distance from the Assyrians and that
        pesky voice. And so, I signed
up for a freighter cruise, and when
the crew had all the cargo loaded,
        we set out.
I was fast asleep down below, relieved
to be going in the opposite direction,
when the sailors awakened me, terrified.
There was a tremendous storm, and
        the captain was dumbfounded
by both my relative calm and what to do
        with this ship in the storm.
In hindsight, perhaps I should have left
the part about running from Yahweh
        out of my account.
When mad rowing and throwing cargo
overboard failed, they had little choice but
to take my suggestion of bailing me
        into the sea.
And so, they did. The waters calmed,
        and I was fish bait.
Was death preferable to going on
mission work among the Assyrians?
        My fate seemed certain regardless.

What came next can best be described
        as unceasing prayer.
Out of the belly of Sheol I cried,
and Yahweh heard my voice.

        My spirit was resurrected, and
my life was spared when that big fish
spit me onto the shore from near
where I had tried to flee. I made

haste to Nineveh and preached to
its people of their impending doom.
     My work done, I sat back to watch
the destruction. I imagined what it
might be like to see Yahweh consume
such a large city in very short order.
     Yet across the city,
people were putting on sack cloth
and ashes as a testament to their
     evil. Even the king
came out of the palace and declared
a time of fasting and praying. He,
too, in sack cloth and ashes.

Gifts not accompanied with a heart of gratitude,
however divinely endowed,
     can be poison to the heart.
Yahweh had shown mercy to Nineveh.
Yahweh had shown mercy to me in
the belly of that big fish. As I had believed
     all along, Yahweh is merciful.
I looked the fool telling these foreigners
that their destruction was imminent.
How long would they remain repentant?
     About as long as I was grateful
to have my life back. My irritation
made for unpleasant words
between me and that voice, lurking
     around my shade tree.
In the heat, she clipped its life, and
there I was, hot under the collar and
     under the sun.

I would like to say I had the last word.
     I had no comeback.
Sure, I could have found a grateful heart
     for Yahweh's mercy to Nineveh

and went on to the next tent meeting
        in the next evil town.
A real poet would have done just that,
        hopeful to be an agent of mercy.
At least I might have been left to ponder
        the lost and confused
and how Yahweh cared for these foreigners
        and their animals.
I might have taken that tack. I did not.

All that was left to do was to try again
        to make it across that sea and hope no
transport by big fish was involved.
        Destination Tarshish.
Great Voice, leave me alone!

The Poet Amos

We are unlikely vessels. The
    palace and the temple
prefer their paid and controlled
prophet class to develop the
    narrative of the empire.
They use all manner of
flowery language and justification
for war and wealth to market
to the people justification for
why they live in splendor and plenty
    while others have nothing.

When we poets come along, it is
    most inconvenient
to their agenda. Poets seek truth
and care little about offending
the top percent who
    control the economy.
It may be detrimental to our life span
    and can certainly bring those
powers crashing down upon us.
    But at the end of the day,
we honor the poetic
tradition of speaking truth to power
while, at the end of their day, their
    unequal scales tilt
evermore to injustice and greed.
They ooze with corruption and
sleaze, all the while dressing it up
    in finery only they can afford.
Selling the lie that they have our best
    interests at heart.

    I was a simple man
who kept a small herd and tended

the few sycamore-figs around my farm.
As you will have gathered, the temple
would not recognize me as their
        credentialed, professional
prophet. I was all too glad to
make that point for them.
        Poets aren't for sale,
and we don't come out of the
        ranks of the powerful.

        I lived in a time of great
economic disparity. My own
small farm allowed me some
delicious meals of meat with
figs, and I could have gone about
        my daily life, kept quiet, and
ignored what was going on about
me. This level of complicity
        ate at my soul.
Across my country, the desperation
of the poor was growing. The
injustice of the palace and temple
        was blatant and perverse.

The temple was at the center
of the corruption. They were big
on pomp and circumstance. They
        loved elaborate rituals and
sacrificing animals on the altar
and men, women, and children
for their warring economy.
        They shouted out their
nationalistic pride as some
        breastplate of honor,
when all it really was was bravado as distraction.
        Every policy was set to make
the measure to the poor smaller

so that the rich could amass the shekel.
        Enough was never enough.

If Yahweh is a god of justice, then
one must look at the injustice of our
time and ask what can be done.
        As Yahweh abhors
injustice, so it must follow
        that Yahweh's law of all Creation
must force that injustice to
ultimately be overcome. That
seemed more dream than reality
in my days.
        But the dream persists, just
as the free gifts of Creation persist.

        That our leaders act willfully
against this natural force of
what is just can only mean that
their kingdom must be labeled
        for what it is. Evil that
supersedes a land flowing with
milk and honey for all. How Yahweh
        will usher in such a final
peaceable land, we poets do
not know. We write in imagery
to open the imaginations of others
to grasp the evil and conceive of the
        possibilities for good.
It will only dawn when we awaken
        to its possibility.

For the poet to abide in silence
in a time of injustice is not possible
        without one's
        complicity in the system.
This simple farmer made that

choice easy enough.
I had to speak for the poor.
For their dignity. For justice.
That justice and dignity
shall one day roll down like waters,
and righteousness
like an ever-flowing stream.
This is the God I know.
The shekel. The sword.
These are the idols.

The Poet's Wife

My life seems both strange
    and surreal.
I was enslaved by one of the
local pimps. No sugar-coating here.
    Let's keep it real.
    I had no life of my own
other than being used one moment
and judged the next. I had few
expectations for the future other
than to remain in this state until
    tossed aside soon enough.
What came after that, I hoped,
would be an early death.
    Not much of a life.

    I say my life was strange
and surreal not because of my
time spent as a enslaved prostitute, but
because of what happened next. Quite
out of nowhere. I thought this man
    must just be another 'John.'
As it turns out, he didn't conceal
his identity. In fact, throughout
all that was to come, he let the
whole world know. He knew how
to get attention! This man,
    the poet Hosea,
bought me from the pimp and
took me home to be his wife.

Living with a poet isn't easy.
    Temperamental, looking for
metaphors in every daily happening,
putting it all out there—these
seem to be the norms one

must live with when married
to a poet. He seemed oblivious
      to the obvious shame
that he should have felt marrying
a prostitute. No, to him
our marriage was full of symbolism.
As he was the faithful husband,
I was the image of unfaithfulness,
      loved in spite of myself.

      And he did love me.
At least in his own peculiar way.
I could have done with a lot less
      public attention.
But there was no escaping the past,
      and, rather than try,
he made our marriage fodder
for his poetry. He didn't stop at me.
      Each of my children
were named so as to suggest sympathies
      to his narrative as well.
He the ever-faithful. Me the at-risk
transgressor. The kids metaphors for
      what was to come.

      I could never really love him.
I hope you might understand at least
      in some small measure why.
In part, I could never dismiss that I
was bought for so many shekels. And
by the laws of land, underpriced at that.
      Being vulnerable
doesn't give one much power over their
destiny. Mostly, my life was better.
      I will concede that.
I wouldn't be put out at the end of my
usefulness, as my previous owner was

sure to have done.
But neither can I say that I
    would ever know dignity
in any meaningful measure.

I don't condemn Hosea for this.
    We lived in a time of
black-and-white legalism.
He risked no small degree of
ridicule for taking the likes of me
    for a wife.
Still, I longed for a time when someone
    could offer me
transformative compassion.
    When a man could look at me
and the crowd and see no difference.
    When dignity and mercy could
flood my soul!

The Poet of Moresheth

I was perhaps the first but certainly
    not the last
to see that the path we were on
was going to be our destruction.
    Specifically here, I am speaking
to the destruction of Jerusalem.

(I did speak boldly to the broader
destruction of Judah as well.)

I lived in a time when the
leadership put a city beautification
project in place that was not
financed on the taxes of the rich
    but that hit the commoner
hard. Very hard. The rich enjoyed the
growing splendor of their class
divide, while the poor only
    suffered more and more.

As usual, the prophet-class, those
paid-for seers, painted a rosy picture
that validated the exploitation
narrative. Nothing new there,
    but I wasn't shy
about calling them out.
They would speak about peace
    on their full bellies while
ready for war against the starving.
    All the while extolling,
"Surely Yahweh is with us!"
    I think not.
Well, Yahweh in faithfulness was
indeed with us, but we were
    far from Yahweh—

far from the Covenant
in thought, word, and deed.

Gloom and doom was not
my message, despite the destruction
that seemed imminent to me.
    The broken Covenant was
a serious matter. But the Faithful One
would not break Covenant, and
    so it was I lived in hope.
It can seem hopeless. Everywhere
I looked I saw justice perverted,
    bribery, and violence.
It was systemic suspicion and division
    right down to the household.

It seems so simple, really. Peace, that is.
Why is it so hard to honor the
basic tenants of the Covenant that
    promises unity with Yahweh?
To honor justice uncompromised?
    To have a heart
towards mercy over judgment?
    To walk humbly
with no place for pride in our lives?
This is our path to peace, however
    overgrown it may look now.

The Great Voice breathed her
words of hope to me,
    and I listened.
She spoke of a Peaceable One
who would come one day to our
    ancient town of Bethlehem.
A Peaceable One who would
care for and feed his flock to the
    ends of the earth.

Yes, not just our few people,
    but all!

But before that day, I believe
we will know destruction, misery, and
violence. For these are the seeds we
have planted. And first, we must reap
    what we have sown.
It is for each of us to sow the seeds
of peace. For my part, I cast
    those seeds
    along every path I trod.
Granted, among a seemingly mighty
    monoculture crop of violence.
Still, the hope endures.

The Adversary

In his darkest moments, the
    poet Jeremiah
cursed the day of his birth.
He cursed the man who gave his
father the news of his birth,
"Because he did not kill me in the womb,
    so my mother
would have been my grave. Why
did I come forth from the womb
    to see toil and sorrow
and spend my days in shame?"

    That may sound over the top,
but I can relate to it perfectly. We
both knew post-traumatic stress well. My
wife pleaded with me to "curse Yahweh
and die." I could lament the day
of my birth, but curse Yahweh,
    I could not do.

    Since the days of Adam and Eve
through Noah, Moses, and the kings,
our people have held that there
    is a cause and effect
between Yahweh's blessings and curses.
    It might be instantaneous death,
or it might be a drama that plays out
over centuries of time as in the
four hundred years of captivity
    in Egypt from the famine to Moses.
But the narrative was the same.
    Sin brought Yahweh's curse.
Right living bestowed Yahweh's blessing.
    Prosperity gospel for the lucky.

The only problem with this
     was that facts on the ground
did not back it up. For one thing,
     bad things happened to
     good people,
and good things happened to bad people.
If Yahweh was paying any attention,
the books of blessing and curse were
     in constant disarray
and certainly seemed to be cooked
     to favor the powerful.
I found myself taking on the system.
My name, Job, means adversary, and I
became an adversary against the
     blessing/curse narrative.
Honor and shame are really the
narrative of empire, and imposing
this system on Yahweh, I believed,
     was of our doing.

The story is well told of how I had
everything one day, but soon enough,
     my life was in shambles.
What had I done? Whatever it was,
family and friends were persuaded
     my sins were of such magnitude
as to bring this doom upon myself,
     having stirred up Yahweh's wrath.
I stated my case again and again.
     I was innocent of
such an offense against Yahweh.
Back and forth we went, my friends
trying to box me into the blessing/curse
narrative, and me pushing back
     mightily against it.
I may not have understood the why,
but the Spirit within me pushed me

to repudiate this doctrine of
  Yahweh the Avenger.

I wished I could say this all led
to much-needed clarity on suffering.
  Alas, such was not the case.
I did receive some vindication. It
was not my sin that had brought my
  life to ruin.
And it was not my great virtue
that restored it. The restoration came
in great measure as mysteriously
  as the ruin.
For Yahweh's part in all this, the
  Great Voice
carried on a great deal about who
I was to think I could comprehend the
  complexity of the cosmos
and Earth's great Creation.
  I was not there
when the foundation was laid,
so how could I hope to understand?
  This was true.
The greatness of Creation is well
beyond my mind to comprehend.
  In humility, I put on
sack cloth and ashes, knowing I would
  never understand it all.
All I could do was surrender to it.

I wish my story had moved more of our
people to understand my adversarial position
against the honor/shame and blessing/curse
  narrative that the Great Voice
confirmed was not what brought
  calamity upon me.
Bad things happen to good people.

My advice: Love them.
  Don't judge them.
Their calamity might well be
  your calamity.
Have enough humility to ask,
  "Who can understand?"

The Poet Jeremiah

I was but a boy
when I started out. In full disclosure,
my family had a four-hundred-year
grudge against the establishment
since the king, Solomon, banished
our ancestor and priest, Abiathar,
for opposing his assent to the throne.
The paranoid king quickly
slaughtered all opposition. Such
was his so-called wisdom. Killing a priest
was tricky business, so instead of
Abiathar being killed, he was banished.

When the Great Voice
first came to me with the charge
to pluck up and tear down,
to destroy and overthrow,
I resisted. As I said, I was
a boy. I had no discernible gifts
for speaking and no authority
to do so. The pop on the back
of the head came quickly and bluntly.
Quit whining and get to it.

The notion of perpetual enemies never
made any sense to me. Why live under
threat of war or war directly when a little
goodwill is possible? This was
but one basic tenant of my complaint
against the palace and temple leadership.
Another was their gross idolatry.
Their fidelity
to the Covenant of Yahweh
was a joke.

"Search its squares and see if you
can find one person who acts justly
    and seeks truth—
oppression upon oppression,
        deceit upon deceit."
I believed trying to awaken the elites
who were living in denial of the
oppression their consumption fostered
        was my task to do.

(It is all ours with eyes to see
and ears to hear to do, is it not?)

The leadership played foolish games
with Egypt and Babylon. Whether
our fate would fall to poor leadership
or the quest for the empire's expansion
        was hard to quantify.
        Something had to give.
If we couldn't get along with the King
of Babylon and continued to be a
thorn in his side with our military
        and security operations, then
the more powerful kingdom was
going to crush our capital city and
        take captive those who
had played their hand poorly.

I warned them repeatedly about
the destructive path we were on.
The prophet class peddled,
        "Peace, peace. We shall
know peace across the land."
Always the justification for sending
boys off to war. We're just a few
        battles away from peace.
Fight on for peace!

The Great Voice breathed her instruction
for several dramatic acts in an attempt to
    get their attention.
One was to take a ruined loin cloth
and wear it as symbol of ruin brought on
by the pride of Judah and Jerusalem.
    Another time, I carried a large
clay pot out to the gate where a crowd
    was assembled and threw it
forcefully to the ground to
    shatter it in pieces,
as their lives would be shattered.

I wasn't just a voice of gloom,
though be not mistaken, I did paint
    a bleak picture.
    "The sword to kill,
the dogs to drag away, and
the birds of the air and
the wild animals of the earth
    to devour and destroy."
    This was their fate as I saw it.
But I was also a believer in
redemption and reconciliation.
I believed the Covenant was as
true in my day as when Moses first
    confirmed it.
The Covenant towards God
    and towards neighbor:
righteousness, justice, steadfast love,
mercy, and faithfulness.

The Great Voice touched my mouth
on that fateful day and spoke these
words to me as well:
    "You are to build and plant
all that is good in my Covenant."

Between the lies and the idolatry
        was that ever-present,
inexplicable yearning for justice and
mercy. The Covenant remained
the promise despite what seemed the
inevitable destruction and overthrow
        of Jerusalem.

        The destruction came.
I wish I could say that justice followed it
        in a new Jerusalem.
Sadly, it seemed this was not to be,
though I would not live to see it.
        Other poets will have to pick
up the mantle and carry on.

They put me in the stocks
and threw me as good as dead into
        the muck of a cistern,
accusing me of undermining
        military morale.
Sympathizers would help me, but the
powerful would rely on the
        'convenient truth'
of their prophet class, while
my words only infuriated them.

        I may have been a boy
when I started out. By my protests then,
you know I expected there was nothing
I could do. I was wrong about that.
        Giving a life to integrity
and a voice for justice and the poor
        isn't nothing.
I consented to the call.
        The Great Voice gave it words.
        And, as always,

the covenantal Love of Yahweh
    is standing by,
ready when we are.

Isaiah and the Return to Jerusalem

I write as the last of the Hebrew poets
known as Isaiah. The first gave early warning
to the people of the destruction of Jerusalem
    by the Babylonian Empire.
The second nurtured the people with
    hope throughout the time of
Babylonian rule, and I came along
with a poet's voice for what a new
Jerusalem might look like when we
aligned ourselves with the Persians.
    It seems part of our history
is to be passed along from empire to
empire, and we are to never truly realize our
    own destiny as a land flowing
with meat and milk and honey for all.

The priest, Ezra, and I stood in stark
contrast to what should come next as
    we each set out to suggest what the
rebuilding of the city should look like.
Ezra was a man of class distinction.
    He and his priestly class
wanted the same old formula. Strict
legalism on who were worthy of
powerful positions and who were not.

I was decidedly not of this persuasion.
    I was a poet and not a priest.
I'm not saying you can't be both, but
experience shows it to be highly unlikely.
    I believe if the tree is to
stand against the forces that drive
against its life, it must be deeply
    rooted in justice.
And it must welcome the light that shines

upon the good of the created world
with its great diversity. So, for me, the
        new Jerusalem
was a place of great hospitality,
welcoming, and inclusion. The
Great Voice spoke powerfully to me.
        "Do not let the immigrant
say that Yahweh has been separated
from us. Do not let the eunuch
say that we are hopeless and lost."
        If the new Jerusalem was
to usher in a peaceable epoch, then
        the very foundation of the city
must be justice and inclusion.

Ezra took a different view. His
worldview was informed by
        bloodlines and class.
        It must be orderly, orthodox,
and ordained. Eunuchs and
immigrants may be okay as slaves,
but they hardly have any place in
the administration of the economy
or in ritual worship and purity codes.
        In other words, it must be
the same, tired, failed formula
of empire in whatever guise.
        I did my best to speak to
the beauty and grace of a peaceable
epoch, hoping it would get enough
buy-in to at least get a hearing.
        That for once,
we might actually try the covenantal
way of Yahweh. We might give
        neighborliness a chance.

Yet, sadly, Ezra's status quo

of governance methodology
would define Jerusalem then,
    just as it shall continue to do
as long as exclusion and class
    rule the hard-shelled heart.
The paradigm shift towards the Covenant
    remains the hope
while we endure the idols of empire and
    its ever-failing cycle
of violence, greed, and fear.

Book Two: Voices and the Peaceable One

Starry Starry Night

    i. Shepherds
Those clear, moonless nights
when the stars saturate the heavens
    as well as our minds
put us always in a reflective state.

Our little band—our coterie and our
humble flock of sheep—were
settled and content. The small
fire we had built gave us just enough
light to illumine the woolly creatures a bit
and fend off any night chill.
We lay quietly, contentedly, taking
an occasional puff of the cannabis
we had found near the stream.

(No war on drugs had been dreamed of
in our day, even though the empire was
always driven to war for war's sake.)

Small talk was avoided on these nights.
We had plenty of time to lament
    the greed of the politicians and
their crowd of the advantaged
    self-admiration club.
They would not steal our thoughts
on nights like these.

What happened next we couldn't
blame on the smoke or our slightly altered mood.
Out of the night sky we all saw it.
A heavenly creature appeared before us.

It scared the living wits out of us!
Clearly, our fright was apparent.
The creature tried to assure us
    we had nothing to fear.

Nothing to fear? The creature was
apparently ill-informed on the matters of state
under which we struggled for our dignity.

We listened keenly as the creature told
of a birth in a stable. It would seem the
creature did know of our oppression, the assault
on our simple way of life, and the hardships of
our day. For in the telling, we were assured
a Peaceable One had come into our midst.
Someone to finally lift the yoke of empire
from our backs. Coming to this place
in humble circumstance. No regal crown
    to weigh him down.
Just simple, home-spun cloth, a little
straw, and a married couple who had
made the simplest vow there was
    to all that is good.
    "Yes!"

Maybe the cannabis helped, but
none of us thought so. For what
happened next filled our imaginations
with a great divine proclamation
by all the hosts of heaven as it rang out,
    "Peace on earth.
    Goodwill to all!"

We were invited to see for ourselves.
    And so we did.

(One of our band would miss it firsthand.

Someone had to stay with the sheep.)
    We wandered down
the hill and found this newborn
child, just as the creature had said.

So it was that a new history for us had begun.
The re-incarnation of Creation's dawn.
    The gift of love and peace for a
world that was created in love and peace.

We carried that night all our days.
Hope had entered our hearts and would
        never depart.
The empire's power over us lost forever in
        that quiet stable in Bethlehem.

                ii. Mary
The empire had its demands—convenient
        or inconvenient.
It made no difference to them. We tried
to go along as best we could, and so it was
that we headed to Bethlehem. This was our
duty, despite the fact that my own state was such
        that the trip was both risky and hardly
appropriate. Riding on an ass
across those roads when great with child
wasn't exactly prenatal "best practices."

The town was so crowded we couldn't
find any place to take us in. I guess
I was a pitiful enough sight that one innkeeper
finally let us bed down with their
domestic animals. We were glad to finally have
        a place to rest.

By now, Joseph needed it every bit as much
as I. He bore a distinct look of angst and

melancholy not to be unexpected from
a man whose life work was hard work and
a simple desire for the most basic
        dignity of others.
Something he'd given me, despite severe
        risks to his own reputation.

By then, our chance to rest seemed like
        a divine gift,
though, for its crude comfort, it was short-lived.
The child was ready, whether we were or not.

My relatives hadn't quite prepared me for
a stable scenario with only my husband to
help. Carpentry isn't exactly on-the-job-training
        for midwifery.
At least a farmer is used to deliveries.
But what does a carpenter know about it?

Whether he was a master of hiding it
or just excited about the prospect of this
        new life coming into the world,
the angst and melancholy were gone.

He looked at me with such reassurance
that we simply trusted that we'd come this
far in safety and would soon hold
        the promise of the angel
        in our arms.

As dawn approached, a small band
of shepherds appeared at the stable door
and told us of their encounter with
some heavenly creatures. Having had our
own encounters, it was easy to take them
at their word. Why only them?
        The city was oblivious to us.

If the heavenly host had cried out as they claimed,
why was it that more hadn't heard it?
    Solitude has its advantages.
For drowning out good news, there is nothing
like overcrowding in a city, whatever the size.

I found my own solitude with
    the animals,
    the humble band of shepherds,
    Joseph, and
    the boy suckling at my breast.
I closed my eyes and imagined the
emperor's first born coming into the
world in the grand palace of Rome.
    Here we were.
Fulfilling a divine promise from our
own God who had made the message clear:
Peace on Earth is born out of simplicity.

The unglamorous ordinary exemplifies
    all that is extraordinary.
    This was the stable's gift to us.
It was to be for the boy the great calling
that would follow him all his days.

Yes, the empire would put him to a cruel death
that would pierce any mother's heart; it
    certainly pierced mine.
But even in that death, he would offer us all
    absolution for our complicity.
Even in his agony, he would neither judge nor condemn.

For all those who listen still, we hear the words,
    "Peace be with you.
    My peace I give you."

He and I would have a few years together

that for both of us were, in so many ways,
    a continuous epiphany —
for ourselves and for the world.

        iii. Joseph
My own dreams had persuaded me that
the woman to whom I was betrothed was
    extraordinary.
You've heard her account of the days
surrounding our trip to Bethlehem and
the birth of the boy. There is not much
I can add that she hasn't already told.

    Even before the trip,
she made me wonder about our
    patriarchal society.
I was to follow *her* on *her* journey.
I put my reservations aside and did
    just that.
Angels in my dreams tended to offer more
compassion than the temple establishment
    was known to offer.

Another dream would lead us on a sojourn to
another country for a time. I feared the empire
and was convinced by the visitation of the sages
that the puppet Herod would be thirsting for
the boy's blood.

(The empire enjoys spilling blood.)

    When that puppet was dead, we returned home.
The boy and I would take the days as they came.
He would spend many years working side by side
with me while his mother waited for
    me to let go
and for him to get on with it. Knowing the

unkindness of the world for peacemakers
and the hypocrisy of the temple establishment,
    her promptings would be
    no easy concession
to her motherly love. She had taught the boy
    the essence of her own faith:
"Let it be with me according to your word."

This was to be their story, not mine.
The temple wasn't ready for
the likes of her strong will and divine calling,
and she would wander in the wilderness,
    close to him.

I, for my part, would do my part. Perhaps,
in addition to teaching the boy the joy and
dignity of good work, I would be able to show him
    that dignity is a gift to be bestowed
    on those who are otherwise ostracized.
This would be my humble gift to Mary.
    It would be the boy's humble gift to all.

The Grieving Town

i. The Sages
When we set out,
we could not have foreseen
the devastation our visit would cause.
We, doctors of the eastern religious
world, had traveled according
to our astrological charts, following
the star of a new king.

We went first to the most logical place
to look for the newborn.
The palace had no new heir.
Our divine inclinations would
ultimately allow us to understand
the ingratiating king's real motives.
We left the country another
way rather than helping to bait his trap
any more than we
had already done.

We found the new light of night sky
not to be a regal birth at all.
This young family confirmed a new
reality for each of us.
We were there to stand in awe of the
new paradigm.
Humility had overcome pride.
Simplicity had ushered in a way of peace.
Our gift of gold—likely just as quickly
given to those poorer than themselves.

We wish we could have somehow
forestalled the violence that was to come.
As the educated and credentialed
doctors of the East that we were, the

attention we brought to this town
would become the king's obsession.
    The uneducated shepherds had
managed to come and go without
any attention from the palace. Our
higher standing set the ground for
        escalation, much to our regret.
Our visit would turn too quickly from
        joy to anguish.
Anguish for the town and the horrors
        they were about to know.
    Anguish for the boy whose
ultimate fate would be sealed by
        the same small mind of evil.
Anguish for the unwitting complicity
        our simple act of homage would cost.

    ii. The Mothers and Fathers
Our histories are overflowing
with incidents not all that unlike
our own day, where blood was shed
        as needlessly
        as one can imagine.

Until Herod's forces came into
our town with the sole intent of
        killing every toddler and infant,
we had not thought too critically
about the stories of our own God
killing, with mysterious fashion,
        the first-born
        males of Egypt.
We had been passed over and would
be grateful such violence had spared
        our children.
We were not spared now.
        Not in this town.

There was some irony that the
intended victim was spared by
    a flight to Egypt.

We found ourselves consumed
    by grief for the barbarous
slaughter of innocent children.
Through the grief, we wanted
to understand. For the first time,
a few among us began to question
not only the mad king's edict but
our own history of the
    night of terror in Egypt
and the many slaughtered in
villages at the hands of Joshua,
Joab, and others of our people.
    Was this some perverse
divine judgment on us as we had
    held it was for those before us?

Most could never begin to
reconcile any of this. It was
    seemingly needless killing
that would likely forever mark our hearts
    with hatred and fear.
Some would try their best to move
on. Not to forget, but not to really
    remember, either.
Many would hold onto the hate
and support any violence that might
    exact even the least bit of revenge.
For the few who knew our only
hope was to move beyond
    the hate and the fear,
it would be a time of great
reflection on our own complicity in
    violence, war, and murder.

Did God kill the young men
of Egypt as a judgment?
And if he did, was this killing
    by royal decree
    also a judgment?

We were common, small-town folk.
It seemed impossible that we could
deserve such a wrathful punishment.
For the first time, a few of us
    walked in the shoes
of other people in other villages
who had known their own
    wrathful outcomes.

It was not something we could
speak freely about. At best,
it was a silent, solitary pondering
that the few of us were trying
    to untangle in our minds.

A small band of shepherds had shared
their story of a night not long before
this calamity in which they had
been told of a Peaceable One
    born in our town.
They had come here to see him. We knew
    nothing of his birth.
Soon, eastern sages traveled here as
well, looking for a king and finding
    instead the same Peaceable One.
It haunted us that the birth of
a Peaceable One could set off such a
    violent chain of events.
Yet, this seemed to be the case, for
soon after the sages departed, the
    wrath of the king was upon us.

Those of us who pondered our
own grief with all who grieved
before us came to a similar result.
That our "Passover" should, in
any way, celebrate our children being
spared over another father's child,
over another mother's child
being killed, was no longer any comfort,
whether in God's name or the empire's.

We had become the fathers and
mothers of all children. We would
forever grieve the wonted violence
of all inhumanity and its destruction
of human dignity at its core.

Our children would not die in vain.
Revenge and retribution are
endless cycles that fail to transform.
These, our slaughtered children,
would transform our
hate and fear. They would stand
forever as innocents against the
madness of kings and armies.

The Peaceable One would
speak boldly where we had held
our tongues so as not to offend.
The Peaceable One would
one day confirm, with his own
execution, our silent pondering.
"They know not what they do."
Yet we, too small a fragment
of our people, forgive.

Speak, Holy Dove

   i. Simeon
The orthodox leadership doesn't
   quite know what to do with us.
We might well be dismissed out of hand,
but the commoners see integrity in our
discipleship, and the priests, scribes,
and pharisees hope they will benefit
   by proximity.

You have to be awake to see what
   isn't obvious.
They didn't make a grand entrance
   with the fan club in tow.
   No finery in their garments.
They came with the simple intent of
presenting the prescribed two-turtledove
offering of the poor. I don't think
they expected any special attention.
These villagers were in the big city
   for ritual atonement.
My singling them out was not
something that they had anticipated.

I, on the nearer side of the tomb,
was moved by the Holy Dove. I interrupted
their ritualistic duties, took the child into
my arms, and wept as I saw the
   redemption of Israel
incarnate there before my eyes.

Not every blessing starts with,
"Now may your servant
   depart in peace."

   Mine did, for

my eyes had seen God's salvation.
    A light for all and the glory of Israel.

And we must acknowledge that such a
divine blessing isn't normally followed
by the heartache they were sure to know.
    "This child is destined for the falling
and the rising of many in Israel.
    A sword will pierce your own soul, too."

Though really, I could see it only affirmed
what they already knew about the boy.

I had interrupted the prescribed ritual already,
and so, bucking the system a bit that day
    didn't bother me.
I walked out to the portico and
set the sacrificial turtledoves free.
What is the point when you are holding
the promise in your arms and in
    your heart?
Departing in peace.
    Is there a better end?
I set the captive doves free, just as
    the Holy Dove
    has set me free!

    ii. Anna
I knew of Simeon's deepest desire
that before he passed from this life,
he would know the Peaceable One.
    His faith never faltered.
Though for the faith he never
knew for certain that the gift
would be given to him
    in his earthly days.
Yet it remained the hope.

Off in my usual corner where I
spent my aged days, I saw the
    old man brighten
as he saw these country folk
with the boy come into the temple.

    Clearly, the Holy Dove
had given him a swift bop on the noggin
because the old man grabbed
the child from the startled parents
and set off in poetic prophecy.

The Holy Dove no sooner was on
my shoulder as well, breathing her word
    to confirm the moment.

I know the temple leadership didn't
think I'd still be living at eighty-four.
They allowed my gifts so long as I kept my
place. Not surprising for a woman
    of any age.

I was normally content to pray for
the needs as they were presented to me.
But there were those times when
    the Holy Dove
called for my boldness to speak her word.
This was one of those days.

I could see in the looks from many
who wondered what this
    crazy old woman
was going on about. Some days
are for fasting and prayer,
and some days are for
    waking people up!

I went around the temple excitedly
and moved remarkably well for
such an old woman, exclaiming over and over,
"Let everything that breathes praise the Lord!
        Praise the Lord!
        Our redeemer liveth!"

I would not live to see him
        betrayed and crucified.
I wish I could say I didn't see it coming.
But just as Simeon had foretold,
we who abide in the Holy Dove
know too well the cruelty of the world.
        We are realists.
We are not optimists waiting for
things to get better because we want
them better. Nor are we pessimists
        assigning the evil some
        preordained victory.

Simeon and I, these parents, and the boy
        are the hope.
We live with the assurance that
        these abide—
        hope and love.
And the boy, we saw, *was* such Love
and would be the great hope of the world.
As Simeon had proclaimed, the bonds
of clan and temple were broken.
        This was a gift for all.
Let everything that breathes praise the Lord!
        Praise the Lord!
        Our redeemer liveth!

The Boy

It would be a bit of
    an understatement
to suggest that my life was not
extraordinary from the moment
of its conception. But I wasn't
raised to think of myself as
somehow superior.
    Pride had no place
in the house of Joseph and Mary.

When I was twelve, we made our
trek to the festival of Passover in Jerusalem.
    It was a family and community affair.
It was easy enough to get lost in crowd.
The idea of slipping away intrigued me.
I always preferred to hear adult conversation
over rough-housing with boys my age.
    Sneaking off to make mischief
just seemed likely to hurt someone
    foolishly and unnecessarily.
Not my cup of tea.

    Coming from a small village,
I did see an opportunity to perhaps
probe the temple leadership as the
festival wound down. It went in
my favor that they were intrigued
    with a village boy
and what he knew of the Scriptures.
They were especially intrigued that I was
not a rabbi's son but just an ordinary
    carpenter's son.

It also worked in my favor that my family
was well on their way home before they

realized I wasn't with them.
My mother would have liked to
grab me by my growing ringlets
    and pull me out of there.
To my good fortune, it was my father
who came and made apologies to the
temple leadership for leaving me in their
charge those days after the festival.
The man of our house always opted
    for compassion over judgment.

I certainly had ample time to get my
story together. I was my mother's son.
    "Where would I be but in my
    father's house?"
Mother had her own strength, and
I was sure this notion would be
hard for her to argue down.
    It worked.

Though it confirmed the end of my childhood.
When we returned home, mother asserted
it was time to get to work. Clearly, she
didn't think my discernment was all that
mature, as she insisted I work and
learn the family trade and not go off as
a child prodigy rabbi.

I did, and it served me well. To
my parents credit, they allowed me
many years to come into my
    true vocation.
By the time I left the nest, I thought
I had a pretty good idea of how to
start out. Just as my mother had
challenged me on my way, other women
would challenge me, and I would

challenge the temple leadership with their
    prescribed roles and judgments.

I saw it as my life's work to offer
    compassion and mercy
where others offered
    contempt and condemnation.
But I must say, when it came to my own
religious establishment, more times than
not, I could not hold my tongue. The
    hypocrisy was so blatant!

It would be my doom in the end.
The twelve-year-old boy wanted to
learn always. The old men of the
temple cherished their own security
above all else. Oh, they tolerated
    the inquisitive boy!
But they would not tolerate the
radical-uncredentialled-itinerant rabbi
    the boy would one day become.

The Cousin

My mother claims that I
     leapt in her womb
when Mary visited us those
many years ago.
     I don't recall it.
Though for the telling, I'm content
to think that it might have happened.
It certainly had its own role in her
shaping my early days for something
other than following in my father's
footsteps as a member
     of the priestly class.

My father was a good man, but my
mother and I looked with great
suspicion on his peers. They seemed
a little too self-assured of their
     own superiority.
Their piety was nauseating.

For his part, he was struck dumb
for asking an angel what seemed
a pretty reasonable question about
     age and fertility.
This lasted until I was taken as
a child to the temple for my
presentation to the Lord.

(A rite for boys only.)

This would free his tongue, and he
would pour out a great poem
about my life and my vocation.
     Despite his priestly class,
he allowed me to go a different way —

a way he was fully persuaded was
        the Divine leading.

It was a far cry from his world. I would
live a simple, rustic life well
        outside the established order.
I saw water as an excellent symbol
for cleansing us of all of the garbage we
carried willingly or were compelled to
        carry by the legalism that was
        thrust upon us.

        At any rate, I became somewhat
of a problem for the establishment.
I'm sure my father took some heat
from his peers, but he never tried
        to dissuade me from my vocation.

I saw the boy I'd made such a fuss about
        in the womb coming my way.
We grew up in some familiarity,
        him being my cousin.
I went off at a young age to start my
vocation as the anti-establishment,
        radical baptizer.
He had stayed at home working as a
carpenter. I knew he had another vocation.
I didn't know when he would act on it.
        He seemed in no big hurry to do so.
I was in high gear and he in low.

When I saw him coming down the hillside,
I thought, "Aha! He has begun."
The scribes and pharisees who had come
out to observe me had put me in a mood.
        Vipers...
Anyway, it threw me a bit that this cousin

would want my baptism. I said it plainly enough.
        "You should baptize me."
But he insisted, and so I did. The Holy Dove
descended, confirming the start of his
vocation as the Beloved One.

I, for my part, continued to speak truth to power.
The house of Herod didn't take kindly to
my pointing out their adulterous coven.
        And in the end, it would cost me my head.

(Too many emperors, kings, and powers
would see injustice as their own
        perverse, divine right
to bestow on their opposition. The empire
did not approve of radicals pointing out
their multiplicity of evils.)

In full disclosure, I was a little confused
by the cousin's tactics. I had foretold of one
coming who would baptize with fire.
Yes, I expected revolution!
        The cousin seemed more prone
to sit on the hills and talk in poetic
metaphors. He liked to bless all the
simplest gifts of people and Creation.
        I had even heard
that perhaps he'd forgotten us relatives
when I was told he had said
        to a gathering,

"Who is my mother and who are my brothers?"

While imprisoned, I began to doubt.
Who doesn't doubt in these dark,
        stinking cells?
Was I wrong to think of him

as the deliverer?
He wasn't delivering me!

When the word came back, I finally understood.
    "The blind see; the lame walk; the lepers healed;
the dead raised; the good news proclaimed to the poor."

Isaiah's other foretelling of "bringing forth from
the dungeon"' dropped from the list.

Okay, nothing about breaking me out of prison.
    Understood.

I finally saw clearly. He was not going
to baptize with fire. He was far more
    radical than I.
He would love his enemies and bind the
wounds of the weakest. He would set
us free in our own hearts.
    No ritual purification was needed
    in any form.

I came back to that one phrase.
    The dead raised.
My fate was clear, as was the promise.
The royals would have my head literally on
    their silver platter.
    The temple would approve.
Neither would have my soul.

The boy I had known and the man he
would become had delivered the
promise. It just took some of us
longer to see.
    The promise was love
    and not revolution.
Something in my prison cell I finally

understood.

The Deliverer had delivered me.

Peace was mine.

The Tempter

Timing is everything. And when it
    comes to timing, I am a master!
To close the deal, you have to be a
master. The average weak lot can be
tempted without breaking a sweat.
    Just show up at the opportune time,
and voilà, they will do anything I suggest.

Some of the more contemplative types
like to go into the desert on retreat.
    This is not good timing.
They pay little heed to me during those
days, and I wait patiently for them to
    get back to the daily grind.
However, if they stay there for an
extended time, then the silence can
begin to get to them. My stats show
that if they stay forty days or more,
    then I have a shot.
It's worth a try because these types
can be tempted once haunted by their
own thoughts.
    It's my best chance for a sellout.

My calendar reminder pops up.
    The newly baptized carpenter
has been on retreat for forty days.
He is more disciplined than most
and is plenty hungry and thirsty by then.
    I wander onto the scene.
I urge him to think first of himself.
This is all it takes for most.
    "Command this stone
to become a loaf of bread."

"You mock the free gifts of Creation.
I know the true bread of life.
       You can't deliver it."

      Hum, a man of few words.
No ground gained. I move onto
       the "power grab."
This works on big egos all the time.
       "Here are all the kingdoms of the world.
You may have my powers over all of them
       if you worship me."

"You mock the justice of the Covenant.
       Violence, hate, and fear are your powers.
You can't deliver neighborliness."

  Tough nut to crack.
       Two down, one more to try. I'm
not making any progress here. My
       last best hope is to try to appeal to
his vanity. I quote chapter and verse.
Religious types love chapter and verse theology.
       "He will command his angels
concerning you to protect you. On their hands
they will bear you up, so that you will not
       dash your foot against a stone."

      "You mock humility.
All you know is pride and vanity.
You can't deliver inter-peace."

      I've wasted enough time here.
Between the desert and the wisdom
of this guy, I should just move onto
       the temple leadership.
Working them into a frenzy is easy.
They are not going to like this guy one bit.

I can make this work!
Back to the capital city.
I do my best work there anyway.

The Followers

i. The Men
Sometimes someone comes along who
draws you to them well before you have
any understanding why. There had been
    some local gossip
that someone had come to John
who was the promised Messiah.
We weren't sure what that
meant, but we certainly hoped it
    meant liberation.

As best we knew, this was the guy.
It didn't seem very likely, but we
were willing to give it a try. He said,
    "Follow," and so we did.

We'd like to say we spent our short
years with him totally getting it and
setting ourselves up in the process to
    be in the inter-circle
    in this life and the next.

(We preferred this life, but he kept
on about the kingdom of heaven.
We were willing to hedge our bets.)

The truth is, we never seemed to
understand much of anything.
He was often frustrated with us, though he
never once said, "Get lost." He was
    forgiving of our dim wits
about his teachings, both in public
and in private.

Poor Peter. He often bore the brunt

for us. He even called Peter, Satan.
Later he would insist that Peter was going to
deny even knowing him at his darkest hour.
    Not once but three times.
That seemed unthinkable to any of us.
But when it came to recognizing weakness,
    he had our number
far better than we did ourselves.
He didn't seem to get that we were
his "in-crowd." We didn't see any point
in allowing others in. He'd picked the
twelve of us initially. That was good
    with us.

Constantly, these women were hanging around.
    What was up with that?
Fetch your water and go home! This was
our take. Not his. His mother was in
close proximity enough that we usually
couldn't say anything. When she was not,
we would always try to get
    them to go away.

I would like to say we were
    concerned for his reputation.
After all, a single man interacting
    in public
    with so many women—
that was not a good formula for
gaining prestige in the community.

We were hoping to improve our status,
and these women were not helping.
    It was a lost cause on our part.
He would grin and shake his head
as though to say, "If I had to choose
between you and the women, it would

be an easy enough choice."
He was kind enough to never choose.

ii. The Women

Men! I don't how we can give birth
to these chauvinistic creatures. Do their
helpless days when our breasts
are all that stands between life
and death for them not imprint
        something in their hearts?

The strongest among us don't let
        their games
get too much in our way. We have our
gifts, and, better than they, we know
how to use them. And I think
        faith is easier for us.
We know what it is to be vulnerable.
And we know how deep one must
dig to find strength within. We try to
instill it in our sons. Some are more
teachable than others. Most are not
very teachable on this point. They
have to suffer greatly before finding it,
        and some never find it.
Certainly, many mothers never
live to see it. And too many women
        suffer as a result. Men's
combined insecurity and physical strength
        too often crash down on us.

But, we digress.

These men who followed the Peaceable
One looked at us more frequently
        than not with disdain.

A few of us had an eye on him from the days
of the wedding in Cana. He was hanging
out with other young men at the party—
        still working as a carpenter then.
His mother came to get him, telling him
the host was about to be shamed,
        as the wine was running out.

Something was going on with these two.
"Woman, what has that to do with
        you and me?"
She gave orders to the servants as though
what he just said made no difference.
We would understand later. She was
pushing him to leave home—to start
        his true vocation.
He was resisting, though even on this occasion,
he could not resist the mother
who had borne him. She would always
        be a strength in his life, just as
she would become for us.
        He turned the water to wine.
We watched him from that day on,
        and our numbers grew.

(Perhaps he recalled this day when he taught
of the two asked to do a task. One said, "yes"
        but never acted.
The other, "no," and then did. Here, he
was the latter, obeying his mother after the
fact.)

As he picked up his own rag-tag
group of men to join him in his
work, we followed, too, if in
        less immediate proximity.
We were never far away, and we

did what we could to encourage
other women to seek him out.

Many did, and he blessed and touched
them compassionately. A few were
bold enough to challenge him on
      religious norms.
He could be persuaded! This left
the men following generally at a loss.
      There is little to suggest they
ever did awaken to our possibilities.

We would be there for
      his agonizing death.
We would witness his forgiveness for all.
And we would be the first in the garden
on that morning to proclaim
      he lives!

Of course, the men would doubt us.

The Snared Woman

There are a couple things
      I'd like to address.
I'll start with the less obvious one.

Where does this "atonement
theory" come from? I heard, some
time after my encounter with the
      temple leadership and
the Peaceable One, that there were
notions circulating from his followers
that he had to die as a sacrifice
      for my sins and yours.
      This was God's plan.
That does not align at all with my
experience! Was I in pre-plan limbo
or something? I don't recall getting any
temporary stay. If this atonement theory
thing is real, do I need to take my
case back to the powers that be to
      grant me final absolution?
This may seem silly to you, but I
am being serious. The Grace I
knew that day came with no
stipulations—no future promise of
      a grace yet to be bestowed.
There was no hint of God's killing of the
Peaceable One to work it all out
      in the books of the hereafter.
Strange reckoning. Very strange.
      From my own experience, the
Peaceable One was here to change
our notion of God. To end the
endorsement of God the Vindicator,
      spilling more blood
      for legalism's reckoning.

God is Love. That was the message from
the dawn of Creation—lost in legalism,
        was it not?
Just sayin'.

The obvious thing to address is
        where the man was.
You will recall, only I was dragged
to the Peaceable One in an overt
attempt to put him on the spot
as a prelude to my execution by stoning.
        Luckily for me, they wanted to test
his adherence to the Law of Moses.
Without their devious intent, I would
        have been dead in no time.
        Shamed, judged, and condemned.
A favorite pastime of the powerful.
No thought of mercy for the likes of me.
If you want second chances, you'd better
have plenty of money in the treasury.

It was clear that the Peaceable One had
no interest in laws that condemn
        a woman, while the man went on
with no apparent accountability.
I don't think he had interest in *any*
        laws of condemnation.

It's not easy tripping up integrity save for
out-and-out bearing false witness. In
my case, the temple leadership would be
        out-foxed.
You know the story. I need not repeat it.
I close my eyes and feel that great moment
each and every day. Maybe you do, too.
        The gift of life given to me that
day was the gift for all judged and shamed

of all time.
The great love and liberation of that simple
line: "Neither do I condemn you."

Wryly, he added, "Go and sin no more."
My life from that day onward
might not have been devoid
of all sin
as defined by the temple,
which he and I both knew
was sure to be the case.
But *never* would I turn from
the burden made light,
from the gentlest gift I could have known
from the Peaceable One, whose
gift of compassion
changed everything!

I Am the Man

There was a great stigma attached to me
that started soon after I was born.
     It became clear soon enough—
I was blind from birth, and our
culture attached this as direct punishment
     for some sin of my parents or me.
It seems both the temple leadership and
the community held this view, despite
the argument put forward in our scrolls
     by the man Job.
My life would be relegated to begging
as the only means of livelihood available
to me and shame for the weight of sin
     that had brought this on.

The men who followed the Peaceable One
looked at me one day with curiosity about
my condemnation. They asked,
"Who sinned, this man or his parents, that
     he was born blind?"
They did this within earshot of me. If it
was sin, how it could be my sin was perplexing.
     Is a child not born in innocence,
regardless of the sins of the parents? This I
have pondered my entire life with little
     consolation as to its truth.
Though in my heart, I believed it was true.

The Peaceable One gave an answer much like
the Holy Dove had given Job. "This is not
about sin. It is about the divine working
     in this man's life." I began to feel for
the first time that what I had hoped for
     in the innocence of childhood had not
been a vain notion but the hand of Yahweh.

He didn't have to ask if I had
     faith to be healed.
It was as though the innocence that had
been robbed from me by the legalists was
testament enough. With soil and his own
spittle, he coated my eyes and instructed
me to wash in the pool of Siloam by which
     I had begged for so many years.
The world I had never seen came into sharp
focus. People who had known me all my
life questioned if I was someone else.
     Everyone was talking
around me, about me, and through me,
as if what they knew to be true was not.

     "I am the man!"
What is wrong with these people? Had
I really shattered their notion of orthodoxy
to the point of calling into question their
     own blind devotion?
They called out the temple leadership, who
were more wound up about the Peaceable One
     healing on the Sabbath.
They had never cared about me or my parents.
     Why should today be any different?
It was different. As far as they were concerned,
     I had no business getting into their business.
They determined who was in and who was out.
Direct testimony that the Peaceable One's
     great act of mercy
meant nothing to them. My parents feared
them and left it to me, as an adult,
to speak for myself. They knew
this was their vindication as much as or
more than it was mine, but I guess the weight of
     guilt or fear held them down.

The Peaceable One would care nothing about
their chastisement for him acting as he
had on the Sabbath. No, it was their
    false piety—their blind devotion to
legalism and exclusion that he called out.
    When you claim to have all the answers,
you can be sure your sin remains. This
seemed to be his warning to them.
    I surprised myself speaking to the
temple leadership. Their consternation
amused me in some strange way. I asked
them if they wanted to be disciples of
the Peaceable One. This really got
them fuming! They lectured me on their
ordination and the succession of authority
    back to Moses.
Whatever! They protest too much, me thinks!
Predictably, they threw me out, hoping, I'm sure,
    I would fade away quickly.
I had no plans of living a life of seclusion.
    For any who wish to know, yes,
I am the man!

The Gerasenen

    The caves outside our town were the
only refuge for the likes of me. People
didn't want to have to see or deal with
pathologies they didn't understand.
    It was easy to become their scapegoat.
"The scapegoat of what?" you might ask.
    For anything—everything!
For whatever made them uncomfortable.
They tried to subdue me, to keep me in the
caves, but I was always able to break free.
    I had no clothes. This, too,
served to reinforce their treatment of me.
What could be done to help someone as
    possessed as I was?
Whatever possessed me caused me to
bruise myself with stones, no doubt
a symbolic, self-destructive reflection of
what the religious leaders inflict on
    undesirables.
Often what came out of my mouth emanated
from a host of dark forces I seemed to have
no control over. When the Peaceable One
appeared, these voices cried out,
    "What have you to do with me?"
He wanted to know who was crying out,
    somehow knowing it was not really me.
    "My name is Legion, for we are many."
He wanted the legion to leave me.
    "Send us into the swine."

I need to pause the story here to
    talk about these hogs.
Every town and city was dependent on
a symbiosis with the small farmers who
surrounded them. This was instinctive and

holistic in virtually every village.
This was not the case in large towns and
cities. They began to quickly lose their
    connection to the land
    and its people.
These country folk were typically family
farmers who tended well their small but
diverse flocks, herds, gardens, and fields.
    Any thought of caring poorly
for their animals or land was contradictory
    to their vocation.

    There were those in Gerasene who
had lost their symbiotic relationship with the
country folk. They were interested first
    in good returns on their investments
with little concern for anyone or anything else.
A few of the men pooled their resources
to try to sell meat cheaper than the
    farm family could ever afford to do,
with significant profit margins for themselves.
Swine, it was decided, would be one of the
easiest animals to exploit in this fashion.
    So it was, Gerasene had its first
intensive confinement operation with
what quickly grew to two thousand hogs.
    These were tended by laborers
    paid on the cheap.
There is no joy in work done without love.
They couldn't possibly know these animals,
so all they could do was follow
    the investors' guidelines,
which had no concept of compassion. Largely,
these workers found their jobs contemptible.
Their days were spent with the hogs,
    wallowing in excrement.
The dignity of straw beds and mud puddles

beyond any existence these hogs would ever know.
     The end goal was simple:
Fatten them up quickly and slaughter them.

You have to have this context to understand
     what happened in my healing. These
confined animals were half-mad already, just
as any confined creature becomes. This is
not what the Creator intended. Having lived a
confined and fettered life myself, no one knows
     this more clearly than I.

     It remains a total mystery as to how these
demons got into my head. It was as though
I had some strange, multiple personality
disorder. Perhaps some professional
     doctor of the mind
can explain it, though I have my doubts.
     All I know is they left me in equal
mystery as their arrival those many years ago.
     I believe they chose to leave me
and go to that half-mad swine herd
because of the evil way in which they
were already confined. Of course,
as they drove me in madness from my
fetters on so many occasions, so they would
drive these hogs to break from their
     fetters of intensive confinement.
When they did, it would send them over the
edge both metaphorically and literally.
They broke from their confinement and, in
a mad stampede, ran themselves right
     off the cliff and into the sea.
An end to their mad existence, as well
as a judgment for the investors who had
     exploited them for the shekel.

The Peaceable One and his fellow
sojourners helped to clean, clothe,
and feed me. I wanted to go with them.
    Leave this town far behind me.
He asked me to stay and speak out
for compassion. I am a very different
    undesirable now. I became an advocate
for compassionate, mental healthcare
as well as an advocate for animal husbandry.
I hope my speaking in Decapolis opened
hearts and minds to what is possible
    when mercy and neighborliness
are core practices of our needed symbiosis.
    Many are amazed at my story.
No one more so than I.   The Peaceable One
gave me dignity. I would do all I could to
    honor his work
through my work.

The Woman in the Crowd

For twelve years I had suffered.
Doctors could do nothing for me.
No healer had ever healed me.
I had virtually lost myself. I mostly
tried to be invisible. Any, who
knew of my sickness, wanted to make
me invisible. After all, it was always
assumed such afflictions were a
     punishment from Yahweh.

Stories of healing were beginning
to circulate. Apparently, there was
a new rabbi traveling throughout
the region, the Peaceable One, who,
by his healing touch, had restored many
     to full health.
Now, he had arrived in our village.
I decided on my course of action.
With the chaos of people flocking
around him, I would be able to
     remain invisible as usual.
That was my hope. I was sure if
     I could but touch his garment,
I would be healed. After so many
years of suffering, it seemed such a
     outlandish possibility, but something
(call it the Holy Dove, I'm not sure)
     said I had to go.
This was my hour.

It was not easy.
The crowds were much worse than
I had anticipated. I stooped over
as much as possible
while still being able to walk and hold

my balance, and I pushed my way
slowly but surely through the crowd.
    Finally, I was able to *just*
barely touch the hem of his garment.
But just as I was about to slip back and
    escape the crowd, he suddenly
stopped, throwing everyone off
balance. When he said someone
had touched him, I froze. Others
didn't understand. A whole crowd
was pressed against him. What did
he mean someone had touched him?

It was surely the Holy Dove, for she
now said, "It's you! You know it is!"

I did the last thing I wanted to do at
that moment. I made myself visible
to the judgmental world. I fell at his
feet and told how that simple touch
    of his hem
had healed my years of suffering.
I didn't need to prostrate myself
on his account. He reached out his
hands to take mine and lifted me to
my feet. Smiling, he said,
    "Daughter, your faith
has made you well; go in peace."

I would go in peace and with, as you might
imagine, joy and excitement
    and filled with possibility!
For I would never have to be
    invisible again.

The Boy with Two Fish

We get very conflicting messages from
adults. We are either cute and adorable
and the pride of our parents, or
we are great irritants to the
    wisdom of our elders.

    As a child,
just try to put forward an idea that
    is as plain as the nose on your face
and see what kind of response
you get from the over-twenty crowd.

We often can expect a patronizing
response. Sometimes, we are ignored outright.
    Or we are told to go and quit
bothering them. After all, adults are
always busy with important things and
    certainly know what is best.

Children in the country often have
more freedom to roam than city kids.
I was lucky to be one who could roam.
    I was a quiet boy,
yet perhaps a bit precocious.
On the hills that morning very
near our home, I situated
myself near the Peaceable One.
    My mother never let me leave
the house without a meal in hand.
She rarely bothered with anything
too creative. Today, it was two fish
and a few small loaves of bread.
    Her instructions were always
the same: Share with anyone in need.
What she lacked in creativity, she

made up for in generosity.

I heard the men who followed
the Peaceable One fussing about being
out this far from town with no
food. I attracted the attention of one of them
and said that I would be glad to share
my meal with them.

What happened next made me
smile from ear to ear,
full of astonishment and delight.
The Peaceable One noticed something
was going on between me and the men.
He asked one of them, "Where shall
we get food to feed this crowd?"
(Their first concern was money.)
One of the other men knew he had seen me
talking with them.
He offered, in usual adult sarcasm,
"Well, there is this boy with
his five loaves and two fish." I kept my eyes
and smile intently on the Peaceable One.
He looked at me then, too,
beaming brightly—almost mischievously so.
He came over and scooped me and
my lunch basket up into his arms
and bestowed his blessing
on both. You know the story from here.
Well, at least the adult version in its
matter-of-fact telling. I am dropped
from the story at the earliest possible
moment.

The Peaceable One and I
slipped away. He walked me to the path
that led me home. He smiled and ruffled my

hair. "I need to be away on my own
     for a bit," he said.
I just nodded in agreement and
waved as he went on alone up into
the mountains. I stood there until I could
     only see him in my mind.

When I entered the house that evening,
my father asked what I had learned that day,
a question he would ask routinely.
     I said, "Well, I know that, when
put in the right hands, two fish and five
loaves can feed thousands of people."
     My father shook his head and said,
"Boy, you are a dreamer! One day you
will grow up. Go to bed!"

The Canaanite

I was surprised. I'd heard so much about him.
He seemed a little condescending.
Maybe those men he traveled with had
    put him in a grumpy mood.
They put me in a mood and only made me more determined.
    Yes, I dared him—
look beyond the confines of religion.
"Even dogs eat the crumbs
    under the table."
Such a notion certainly caught
his attention. He knew I meant
business, and while the other men wanted
him to ignore me outright,
    he did not.
He took the world as it came,
and it came with me daring to ask
from him what others would withhold.
    "Woman, great is your faith!"
And so it was that we departed.
    I left, assured of my daughter's
restoration, and he left,
    brightly smiling.

James, Son of Salome and Zebedee

We didn't think of ourselves as a
    comic sideshow —
the twelve of us who followed
the itinerant rabbi. Somehow it
seemed our destiny, or at least a part of it.
    My brother John and I did both tend
to think of ourselves as important in the ranks.
We were arguing about which one of us would be
    on the right hand and which on the left
when the itinerant rabbi was crowned
in glory. He overheard us and found
it most amusing that we'd been
found out. Apparently, that was
    neither ours to know
nor his to tell. We liked thrones
and held out hope. Having come from
more well-to-do folk than most of the lot,
    we also felt a little superior.

On another occasion, we were traveling
to Jerusalem and would be going through
    the town of Samaria. These
people were outsiders, which
    left us wondering why
the itinerant rabbi was interested in
stopping there. A couple others went
to see about setting something up.
They met us as we were approaching to
report that the town didn't want us to stop.
    John and I suggested we call down
destruction to consume the town.
(As you might have guessed, we didn't
quite get the whole "peaceable" thing just yet.)

He wasn't amused this time. He just thought

we were dense, and told us
destruction was not on the agenda.
    We all went on our way.

It wasn't long until he was telling a crowd
a story about a man lying for dead along
the Jericho road. A priest and a Levite
passed the man without helping.
(They were more concerned with legalism than mercy.)
    When he got to the hero of the story,
he looked at the two of us.
    "A Samaritan, while traveling, came near him,
and when he saw him, he was moved with pity.
He went to him and bandaged his wounds,
pouring oil and wine on them."

Yeah, yeah. We get it. Make the Samaritan,
who we were ready to destroy, the hero. The
town, having rejected him, didn't seem to
    factor into the equation.

Right down to our Passover meal, when
he was greeted by throngs as we came into
Jerusalem, we and the other boys were
jockeying for positions of prestige.
    That is how clueless we were!
Over the next forty-eight hours, our zeal
for greatness was swapped for fear.
We thought things were culminating
to greatness—the radical baptizer's
    awaited baptism by fire.
Instead, he washed our feet. He
said the night would lead to denial
and betrayal. He asked us to pray
through the night with him. We just
slept. And once the temple guard
    came to seize him,

we ran in fear. One of us would be
there with his mother as he died. The
other would not. Neither of us
could imagine then that we'd be willing
        to wash the feet of others
when the risen Peaceable One would walk
again with us and whose Holy Dove
would breath words of peace and humility
        into our hearts.

The message of the Peaceable One finally
became our message. We would no
longer worry about thrones and
our places near them. We would
        kneel and kiss the feet
of those in need of mercy.
We finally understood this descent
of serving the poor and vulnerable.
Position was less than chaff to us now.
        Our humility was born of
Love's embrace from the cross.
        Our vanity—burned away by
the flame of Pentecost.

The Walking Dead

I must have looked like some kind
    of walking-dead zombie
when I came out bound in burial cloths
from the tomb where I had been put
after my death. I was surprised so many had
    shown up to mourn me.

    Me and my two sisters were a bit of an
anomaly in our culture. We were all adults,
never married and living as one household.
We had nothing against marriage. Somehow
we just ended up contented with our life
as we knew it.
    The Peaceable One was a close family
friend. The three of us cared deeply for him
and thoroughly enjoyed his company.
    Most men had little to do with
women. My sister Mary always wanted to
be in the conversation. As head of the house,
I didn't mind. Why should his friendship
    be only a male-bonding exercise?

My other sister, Martha, was a meticulous
housekeeper and host. Mary, not so much.
    We all enjoyed Martha's gifts—
no question! She was always puttering in
the kitchen, putting together a meal or
lighter fare for all of us to enjoy. Once,
when the Peaceable One dropped in
    rather unannounced,
Martha began scrambling around to get
something together. Mary was just glad to
see the Peaceable One and didn't care if
there was a little disarray around the edges.
    Martha barked at the Peaceable One

to order Mary to come help her.
The Peaceable One, whose appetite was
unpredictable anyway, said, "Oh, Martha,
you toil while Mary enjoys life as it comes."

He might have just gotten up and helped
instead of saying that. I have to live with
these two. We may have made a life together.
    It didn't mean we couldn't squabble
from time to time. Nothing like domestic
chores to get the aggravations going.
    Mary didn't get up and help,
and we just heard the pots bang louder
then before. She might not have been happy about
it, but she was not going to lessen her
        vocation as a doer.

    The final days during my illness were
difficult. The sisters had sent for the
Peaceable One, but there was no holding
out. I was in pain and fading day by day.
    He was not there when I passed.
Martha, the doer, saw that all the proper
preparations were made and friends and family
notified. Mary was lost in grief. When
Martha heard the Peaceable One was
approaching, she ran out to greet him
as well as to chastise him for not coming sooner
        to heal their brother.
He spoke of resurrection. No one was
quite sure what he was talking about. It had
been four days since I died, and the body
        begins its decay back to the earth
soon enough. Martha pulled Mary from
her mourning in the house and headed to the
tomb, as requested. Being her ever-practical self,
she pointed out that rolling the stone away was

not a good idea, as by now I was surely stinking.
   The stone was removed anyway. No stench.
I was commanded to come out, and I did!
   Mourning turned to amazement!

I turned to the Peaceable One and
whispered into his ear.
   "Isn't dying once enough?
These sisters don't know when to leave
   well enough alone."

I, Caiaphis, the High Priest

I have great powers of discernment,
	as every great leader must.
The demands on my time are
unending, as many seek my gifts
of administration and keeping
	our culture and society
securely within the confines of our
	orthodox traditions.

	I am one in a long line of
carefully considered leaders
empowered to render justice
	and assert moral imperatives.
I see my authority as God-given.
Our scriptures assert the authority.
(I can provide chapter and verse if
such proof is needed.)

	Among my duties is to forge
workable alliances with the empire.
	I must put up with all the
political posturing of the emperor's
appointees. It is not easy lowering
myself to these inferior stooges.

I also must put up with the
	simpleminded commoners
who know nothing of systematic theology
and are forever caught up in the
emotion of the moment brought on
	by any charismatic man.
Left unchecked, these men would
bring down the temple and
	our way of life.
Few appreciate the difficulty

of managing these troublemakers.

One was causing particular
problems. I was forever having
the scribes and Pharisees of the
temple and synagogues showing
up at my door to rail on about his
very unorthodox behavior.
    I had not met him, but by all
accounts he was forever drinking
and carrying on with all manner
    of undesirables. He was
openly defying Sabbath laws.
He tried to trick our leadership
into tripping up on the complexities
of our purity codes and statutes.
I could have ignored it easily enough
if it was just the temple-men complaining.
    (They always complained.
    I could tune them out.)

No, the real problem was the
growing crowds believing a
        commoner—a carpenter
        (a Nazarene, on top of that)—
over the authority of the temple.
Their so-called Good Shepherd.
    He had no authority to teach,
let alone set a new policy for our
tradition. This was not acceptable.

The temple council met with me to
discuss the problem on numerous
occasions, never coming to any
consensus on how to
proceed without causing real
        problems with the commoners.

Numbers were protecting him
and only getting worse with
    each delay on our part.

Then, he went too far for even
the moderates among us. He
made a huge scene in the
    portico of the temple,
overturning the tables of the
merchants and driving out the
animals they were selling for
ritual sacrifice. This was a direct
attack on the very essence of our
    authority among the people.
And he did all this during the
    High Holy Days, when many
were in the city for ritual sacrifice.

    That was it! We called him in
with one intent. To end it once
and for all. We tried to get the
palace to help. We needed an authority
who could exercise the death penalty,
    and we needed to distance
ourselves directly from the deed.
    Herod was useless.
All he did was send him back to me.
We were going to have to make this
a matter of both blasphemy against
our tradition as well as treason
    against the emperor.
We pressured a group of our
known loyalists into being ready
to appear before Pilate if need be
    to testify to his tyranny.
Pilate wasn't going to care about our
complaints. We were going to

have to persuade him that to
    ignore the fanatic
would be political suicide.
His superstitious wife might have
    derailed our plan. She was
pressuring Pilate to let him go
    because of some dream.
    (Women!)
The crowd we had assembled raised
a tremendous ruckus in front of
Pilate, and this indeed sealed
his fate. He finally agreed to
    sentence the man to death.

    I would do it all over again.
I have no guilt. No regrets.
We represent a great tradition
    of a great people.
We have suffered injustice at
the hands of foreign powers and
threats to our authority from
    charismatic rabble-rousers,
yet this has not squelched our pride.
    My duty is to preserve
the authority of the temple, to
ensure the greater security of
our people. His followers would
    make wild claims that following
his crucifixion, he would be
miraculously brought back to
life. The so-called witnesses were
people of no standing in the
community. It was easy enough to
dismiss their wild assertions.
    They would go off and form
a new religion and call themselves
    Christians. Good luck with that.

They will find out soon enough
the difficulty in keeping the sheep
in line. They will find my methods
        good enough soon enough.
Time will tell how well they follow
        in the footsteps of their
        "Good Shepherd."
You'll see; they will defend their
        tradition and orthodoxy
every bit as ferociously as I have.
        Mark my words!

The Trusted Betrayer

Young John never liked me.
He thought he had the inside track
on Jesus's affections, but it was I that
Jesus entrusted with our common purse.
I was the most frugal of the bunch, and
    we lived hand-to-mouth
    most of the time.
But thanks to my frugality, we did eat!
It irritated me to see anything lavish going
on, though in truth it had more to do
    with tight finances
than any actual concern for the poor as when the woman
anointed Jesus's feet with the expensive nard.
Couldn't she finance our work rather than
pour expensive perfume on his feet?
    Priorities, please!

But I was trusted by Jesus. To ignore this
is to oversimplify what led to the great betrayal.

I wasn't the only one among us
who thought this man we followed
was going to assert powerful
    opposition to our political
    and economic oppression.
The other boys may distant
themselves from this reality,
but they were no less invested in
the grandeur of such an outcome,
    as we were banking on him
as the long promised leader of our people.

As the crowds around him grew,
it seemed more and more likely
that the showdown was nearing.

All seemed set
as we came into the east gate
and the crowds cheered his arrival.
He even rode on an ass as though
deliberately mocking the Romans
who entered the west gate on their chariots.
    Finally, our time was coming.

Then, at that last passover meal,
everything, rather than coming into
clarity, became completely bewildering.
Here he was insisting he wash our feet—
    going so far as to say
he'd have nothing to do with us
    if we didn't submit.
It was humiliating to watch him.
What is with him and feet?
    What was going on here?

Then, he talked of denial and betrayal.
It wasn't the first time that he picked
up on our confused state of mind or
    our self-importance
that we placed such confidence in—despite
our track record of failures.

There he was telling me about my
own plans to betray him to the temple guard.
    He didn't elaborate on the details,
but he clearly knew I was taking matters into
    my own hands.
I had no notion that this would lead to
his punishing death! I was certain it was
the next card to be played so that he would
capitalize on the crowds assembled for the
Passover and finally proclaim his
rightful place as king of our people.

Yes, I was trying to manipulate the situation.
    I wanted action.
We would all be well-placed in
    the new world order.
Even then I assumed his awareness of
my plans was a kind of approval. It
gave me the the courage to
    get on with it.

I thought I was following a great
revolutionary. I, along with my
comrades, failed to grasp the upside-
down vulnerability that would
    finally be reveled
in his true form as the forgiving,
    Peaceable One.
Oh, he tried to tell us, but
when you want power and are tired
of oppression, talking peace and love
seem more like crowd pleasing
political tactics than a new way
of living in this world.

    In the garden that night,
when the soldiers arrived, I saw
a submission from him that
pierced me as forcefully as a hot poker
on my chest. I hadn't forced his
hand into the call to action of
    a revolutionary.
He was submitting to their authority.
His one request—put down the sword.

    What was going on?
I found myself going mad.
I didn't want him tortured.
How could things go so wrong?

Weren't the crowds cheering him in the streets
    just hours before?
Where were they now?

Now, he was alone in his hours of torment.
    And I was alone in mine.
That cursed purse! I thought I could
wangle the temple out of some silver
to make a good showing of my intent
    when my real intent was
to upend them in their own game.

    Oh fool!
All those months he taught us, and
I had completely failed to grasp
everything he taught. The women
got it. We dumb men can't see
anything but power or the lack thereof
    in the here and now.

    Oh fool!
    I am lost and alone.
I have made my life excrement.
Forgive me gentle Shepherd!
    I crucified thee!

The Wife of Pilate

My real story is barely recorded.
You might find it not believable,
    but so be it. I must tell it.

My husband was a cog in the Roman
machine. Don't let his title as
Prefect fool you into thinking that
he was a man of his own mind.
There were always opportunists
waiting to pass back to Tiberius
    any fodder available.
Being Prefect of Judea was hardly
a choice assignment, but those
opportunists welcomed any stepping
stone to Rome they could find.
    He had come to this position
more on merit than most. He did
have some heart for justice, even
if Rome pulled the strings of
    injustice as often as not.

Ruling in this part of the empire
    meant dealing with Caiaphis,
the high priest of the Jewish temple,
and his many minions. My
husband had little use for the man.
    I had no use for him.
He seemed to me the conniving kind
of man who would sell out his
    own mother for
a drink in the trough of power.
In their high holy time of Passover
when he came to my husband with
an alleged case of treason, I was
    immediately suspicious.

He could not have cared less about
treason against Rome. Something
was going on. A few inquiries from
our servants confirmed my worst
suspicions. They talked of a
Peaceable One who had arrived in the
city and had gathered a large
following in the last couple years.

(Anytime you want to know what is really
going on, talk to the poor or enslaved.)

This had everything to do
with the temple and nothing to
do with Rome. That was clear to me.
    This troubled picture haunted
my dreams. I shared this with my
husband. He was anything but
dismissive. He confirmed that he,
    too, knew this was a set-up.
What he could do about it, he wasn't
sure. But he would try.

Neither of us counted on the
crowds the temple leadership
was able to muster to testify
    against this man's treason.
They were out for blood, and if
it wasn't the Peaceable One's, they
would see to it that Rome had my
husband's blood. In the end,
he yielded to political expediency,
    but not without his own
    public act of defiance
against those bearing false witness
    against him.
He would use their own purity

code as a testament against them.
Standing before the crowd, he
washed his hands, saying, "This man's
        blood is on your hands."
He even insisted that the soldiers
who had carried out the deed tack
their assertion of blasphemy
and tyranny on the cross.
        "King of the Jews."

I was grief-stricken for our part in it.
        The afternoon of the execution
I spent alone on the roof terrace.
The sky was ominous, and the earth
        shook with many tremors.
It was the eeriest day of my life. My
husband spent the time in solitude
as well—locked in his chamber.
His instructions were clear: No one
        was to enter, not even me.

He had given instructions that
        after the death,
there were to be soldiers at the tomb.
        He was concerned some
of the ruckus crowd would not
        let the man rest in peace.
He did not want to see the man's
head hanging on some post inside
the city, mocked and ridiculed,
        even after death.
        I shared with him something
one of the servant girls who knew
of the Peaceable One had shared with
me: She believed he would
        rise from the dead.

Unbeknownst to me until later,
    my husband had told the soldiers of
both his concern for the body
being desecrated and the
    resurrection rumor.
Caiaphis wanted his own guard.
My husband put his foot
down firmly and made it clear
they were not to be anywhere in
sight. "You wanted Rome to
handle it. Rome will handle it."

My husband had done more than he
could ever claim. For among his
instructions to the soldiers was
    "Should the King of Jews walk
out from the tomb, do not be
dismayed. See to it he passes
    safely from the region."
All the talk of them falling asleep
was part of the cover, should it happen.
    He'd see to it no charges were
ever brought against them that could stick.

History is carefully crafted by
whoever tells the story. For my part,
I hope what little we did might
    bring us some mercy.
Not that we are deserving, for
we could not forestall the inevitable,
miserable death of the Peaceable One.
    But if the servant girl
was right about this man, his
compassion could extend even to
those who would kill him. And one of
the soldiers who carried out the
execution reported back that

he looked out and spoke these
amazing words: "Forgive them."
    The soldier who told us this
added, "Surely this was God in
some remarkable human form."
    All I said was,
"Yes, I'm sure of it."

The Cyrenian

I was just a dark face
standing along the road that day.
      I was no one in particular.
I didn't know any of the three
passing by in their spent flesh.

The eyes of each bore a different
story. The first had the eyes you'd expect.
      Filled with hatred.
      Full of contempt.
There was no remorse to be found as
he trudged up the hill toward his ultimate fate.
He carried the cross with the same resolve
as he carried the lifetime of resentment that defined him.
It was just one more ugly hump on his back.
The last man had a different look altogether.
His eyes were filled with the remorse of
      a lifetime of regret.
He walked on as though the burden he
carried was a just and fitting end to a life
squandered by bad choices and hopelessness.
Up the hill he walked, wishing he had one
more chance to set things right—
      to take a different path.
Not knowing then that such a chance would come.

If there were those in the crowd who knew either
man, they gave no indication of this. These two seemed to
be walking the solitary path of isolation and loneliness
      common to the condemned.
It was the Man between the two who bore
a look I'd not expected. There was no hatred
or contempt and not a single flicker of regret.
Broken, bleeding, writhing in pain, His face
bore only love—His eyes absolution for

us all. I'd never seen forgiveness in the
    eyes of the suffering
    that I saw in His that day.
With all the women wailing and the mockery
of the twisted briar embedded in His skull,
the guilt of the Man to deserve such a death
seemed impossible—a ludicrous mockery of justice.
    Guilt does not know
the innocence we all saw that day.
Some of the soldiers knew it, too. You could see that
the bidding they did for the empire was twisting
their faces into hard, crusty masks of blind
devotion—unsure of the punishment they were inflicting to
this mixed lot and all the mixed lots that had
    preceded them. Year after year of
killing the unjust for justice's sake.
The judgment of man laid low by
extracting life for life, or the blind bidding
    of the powerful
    against the weak.

Yes, I was just a dark face in the crowd—
the type power bids to carry any
heavy load for their convenience. But that day,
it was not a burden at all.
    That gentle Man's cross
was the world's reconciliation-incarnate
across my strong and able shoulder.
Could I have had a higher purpose than to
    take up His cross and follow?

You would not know my name save
for His gentle touch of my hand as they laid
    His cross on me.
Kindly, He looked into my eyes and spoke a single word.
    "Simon."

The Arimathean

I didn't really fear death, and perhaps
that is why I had prepared my own tomb
   well in advance.
Some of us bear witness to our faith
by being there for those who fall to pieces
when a loved one dies. And plenty
do without ever dealing with
   the inevitability.
Well, that is not me.

I lived a comfortable life, and I had
   gone along to get along
enough, the Roman authorities
preferred me over some of my
colleagues on the temple council.

That is not to suggest this was a
virtue of mine. Wealth doesn't come
without some complicity somewhere.
Maybe what I did next was for some
absolution. Humble contrition for
   having it better than most.

I was not so blind to the powers of
Rome or the temple leadership to
not see the injustice perpetrated
on the itinerant rabbi who was
   stirring up the city and region.

The bloody injustice of that day
   called me to action.
I could do nothing to spare his life.
At least I could give some dignity
to his body for the sake of those
   who loved him.

Including me.

Pilate obliged with my request.
With help, I wrapped the corpse
in a shroud and applied burial spices
    as the women grieved.
The tomb was sealed, the soldiers on guard.

Killing the innocent can make
    one paranoid.
I'm convinced that is why the
Roman guard was ordered to stay
at the tomb. I resented their presence,
but I would come to be thankful for it later.

When the women came back
following the Sabbath to continue
    their ritual anointing, they
found the soldiers asleep and the tomb
empty. Had the soldiers not been there,
I suspect I would have been next up
    on the cross.

As it was, the accounts of that day
vary. I can't tell you firsthand what
happened. But, for what it's worth,
I did see what looked like Mary of Magdala
in the garden talking to someone
who was not my gardener. I hastened
from the house to see what was happening.
    By the time I arrived,
    both were gone.
The tomb was empty.
The soldiers had fled.
    The garden was immaculate
and ablaze in blossoms as though
    touched by the hand of God.

Oh, Thomas

I get off easy in many ways.
Betrayal leading to death carries
a far greater stigma than wanting
  evidence to back up a claim.

When the others were afraid of
going back to where the itinerant rabbi
had nearly been stoned, I was quick
to suggest we all go and be
  willing to die with him.

(I have my fearless moments.)

I don't know whether Judas knew
that his kiss would lead to death.
I'm more of the mind that he
thought this would force the
  itinerant rabbi's hand.
He would boldly push back
against the temple leadership.
  Maybe Judas was just in despair
for what *was* instead of what
  he'd hoped *would be*.
It is easy enough to find oneself there.
He wasn't alone expecting some
  baptism of fire—some revolution.

I have great pity for Judas. Death
did not surprise me. The showdown
was brewing—no question. Judas got
caught up in something that might
  have pulled in any one of us.
(Some people seem to live life by the
  draw of the short straw.
Judas was one of them.)

When the end came for the itinerant
rabbi, I thought it was just that—
        the end.
The women would grieve, as was the
custom. The men would press on
in whatever semblance of normal life
they could foresee for themselves.
        Me included.
We were often confused by what
the itinerant rabbi tried to teach us.
Never more so than with his
        apocalyptic references.
If we couldn't get it, what chance
        did the crowds have?
As best I could surmise, death on
the cross was it. It was over.
Judas, too, was dead. The rest of us
        in a daze of sorts.
What we would make of it all,
        only time would now tell.

One trait I possess in spades is that I don't
like being duped. I'm a "facts on the
ground" kind of guy. When I say
I get off pretty easy, it is because I think
        more than most share this trait.
I raise my eyebrows and wrinkle my forehead
        to the gullible, question their good
sense, and completely tune out the
propaganda of the temple and the empire.
        Don't make claims
        without proof.
(Just because you say it's so doesn't
        make it so.)

This doubting Thomas wanted to
        see it to believe it.

When the moment came,
I didn't have to touch the wounds.
    They touched me powerfully!
There, standing before me, was
    the one I'd given up for dead.
The emotional weren't imagining things.
I finally understood. I was standing
    before the Peaceable One.
Now, the pieces fit together in an instant.
    He was the temple that would rise.

You can be grateful to me. I wasn't
    rejected for my doubts.
It was confirmed that day. Some of
us need to see. Some find a way to
hold to the mystical presence through
    a faith I don't fully comprehend.
Theirs—an epiphany. Mine—a persuasion.
The risen, Peaceable One's blessing
    abides with us both.
And for my part, I am hopeful
that Judas abides in the blessing as well.
    How can he not, when there is not
even an iota of chastisement in the risen
Peaceable One for our weaknesses?
We all might have done more in those
final hours. Where was my willingness to
    die with him then?
Judas's kiss may have betrayed Love.
    Love never betrays and never dies.

147

A Parting Reflection

My thirty-three years here went by
quickly, and the last three, in which I devoted
    all my efforts to my true vocation,
were wonderful and terrible, often filled
with joy and, too often, sadness.
    I get it.
The human condition is something else!
    As the poets of old spoke over
and over, the few consumed with power
and control make misery for the many.
    Nothing has changed.
It's the rotten fruit of free choice.
    The obsession with war and violence,
both horrific and pathetic,
confound me. Why does evil remain
    such an attractive option?
It is nothing but ugliness, hate, and fear.
I am the latest voice and the latest hands
    to reach out to the poor, the infirmed,
and all the voices who cry out in their
    oppression.
Ensure I am not the last.
    Speak!

You may think I possessed some crystal
ball in which I could see clearly and
consistently the one I have called
    my Heavenly Father.
As though I am somehow hard-wired to God, and
that each time I prayed, I heard the voice of God.
If this is what you think, think again.
As it is for you, as it was for my mother,
    our lives are a walk in faith.
I trusted, more than most, perhaps, that
within me was the image of the Creator.

Yes, I believe I was an incarnation of the
Divine Presence, but I don't believe trying
to parse the human and divine was mine to do;
it most certainly is not yours to do.
There were plenty of times I felt distant
    and even abandoned.
If I am to understand humanity,
    how could it be otherwise?
Much may be made of my suffering.
    Make no mistake; it was terrible.
But the horrific nature of that experience
is not uniquely mine. The very point is to determine
how common to the human experience suffering
really is. "My God, my God, why have
you forsaken me?" is the cry of all humanity
in these dark hours of anguish and pain.
    My suffering was intense but brief.
Many suffer years of indignity and misery.
    I could not end this.
I can only suffer with you.
    Weep!

I am attributed to many miracles, and
I said that you would be emboldened to do
    far greater things than I.
    This, I suppose, confounds many.
"Say to this mountain, be thrown into
    the sea, and it shall be so."
(I have a sense of humor, too! Some have
so little faith that they can barely get out of bed
in the morning, let alone move mountains!)
    Okay, I had my poetic and metaphoric
moments. I thought this would be clear
enough since many of my teachings were
metaphors, plain and simple. The legalistic mind
wants certainty and literalism. That doesn't
deliver inter-peace and doesn't make for the

149

neighborliness inherent in the Covenant.
    I came not to dismantle the Covenant
but to fulfill it. This was not hocus-pocus.
My spilled blood was not a transactional act but
        a transformational one.
When I offered absolution from the cross,
this was my life validating the Covenant.
The Covenant is not a set of laws to be adhered to.
It is a life of love to be lived.
    Nothing can separate us from Love,
no matter how far we drive ourselves into
madness and despair.
    Hope remains where there is mercy.
Hope thrives in forgiveness and
reconciliation. My peace I give you,
not as the world gives, but for which
        you are called to give, and give,
and give some more.
    Give!

My mind went in all the directions that
        the human mind takes a person.
I've even been known to cuss out a fig tree for
not bearing fruit when I would have liked
to have had a few figs to snack on as we
        traveled down the road.
    My own reflection of this reaction
was to tell a parable about a patient servant
who encouraged a land owner to give
him another season to work rich compost
into the soil and see if, the next year, it might
        bear fruit.
If not, then he would cut it down and throw
        it into the fire. He promised to be attentive,
and the owner agreed to the servant's plan.
This is a good reminder to me—good
stewardship always requires patience.

The right balance of nourishment and
  the wisdom to know
when to resign it to another fate.
  It's also a good reminder for you:
An empty stomach can make one grumpy.
  Cultivate!

The poet in me could not resist calling out
the undue burden of the law and the hypocrisy of
the temple leadership. Forgiving your enemies
is not the same as being complicit with them.
  Always forgive. Never be complicit.
This might be the hardest lesson of all.
  Yes, I'll say it again:
  Always forgive. Never be complicit.
One can appear to be peaceable and still be
  complicit with evil.
The empire and legalists will do everything they can to
  ensure you are complicit.
They will do everything possible to entangle your
security in their agenda of exploitation.
They will boldly claim to speak for the majority.
  My brothers, you are often blind to this.
You followed me in hopes of being part
of some great revolution. Oh, how I
wanted you to understand the antithesis
of revolution! When I washed your feet,
perhaps it finally began to open your hearts.
  My sisters, your powerlessness
among the political boys' club gave you
insights into experiencing the teachings I offered,
  and because you often did understand,
you naturally pushed me forward.
  What great joy this brought me!
But, my sisters, beware: If you sell out to
  the power grab,
you, too, will see life as a battle, greed as virtue,

and yourselves as warriors. You will have
lost the openness you now possess through
        your inherent dignity and humility.
Do not forfeit your maternal gift of
        life-giving sustenance. Let the men
learn from you. Don't follow their path!
I have shown you the way to truth and life.
        Lead!

To all, I hope you noticed what a poor
        chapter and verse
doctrinal theologian I am by intention.
The scrolls are living, breathing words,
always seeking to draw closer to the Word but
        always falling short. This is why I taught,
        "You have heard it said, but I say..."
I'd rather you challenge the most ardent
doctrine for the sake of love rather
than ever holding to tradition for the sake of
        those hard and bound consciences.
They enslave generation after generation.
        Liberate!

        That I could offer the outcasts, male and
female, uncompromised dignity, mercy,
and compassion was, without a doubt, my
greatest gift to give. Understand that
these are not my sole property, but
        the property and call of all.
The poets and I have taught you this. To ignore
this is to consign to evil that which does not
        belong to the evil powers.
There will be those who not only fall to this temptation,
but embrace with pride and endless bloviating,
mocking the free gifts of Creation,
mocking the Covenant, mocking humility.
        These make hell incarnate.

They kill, plunder, and burn for the shekel's sake.
They make endless promises of peace
and prosperity. They boast of their greatness
and of making the empire great, which is somehow
supposed to make us think we are great for being
part of it. Do not believe the lie.
It is always a lie.
If what they do—if what you do—does not reconcile
with the simplicity of the dawn of Creation
when all was blessed as good, then
you know it is a lie yet again.
Would that you would walk naked and
unashamed in the beauty of this celestial orb.
It is heaven if you could only know this.
Awaken!

Though I go now, the Holy Dove will be with
you to breathe our Word unto you. The empire has
done its worst and cannot prevail
against my love, forgiveness, and compassion.
It is for you to carry on, in your fullest
humanity, the work we have begun. When
I am gone, do not worship me! Honor me
by honoring the very gifts of life. By being
co-creators with me
in creating here what you imagine it is that
heaven is like. For the work is to create with us
heaven here and now. My short life confirms
to me the enormity of the task. But my time here also
confirms it is within the human heart and mind
to make it real.
It is not to be dismissed for its difficulty.
Imagine!

Do not make me into a religion. I am not
doctrine and dogma. The legalists will want to
take you there. Emperors may even demand it.

Resist them.
For the Spirit blows where She will, and you
cannot confine Her within your walls,
    your laws, or your scrolls.
I have made you disciples, not dictators.
    Serve in love and humility,
just as I have served in love and humility.
Gather with those around you. Break bread
together. Welcome the stranger. Protect the
orphan. I know you know what to do.
    Act!

Finally, remember when I breathed my first breath
    as your Incarnate One,
the Word of the divine messengers
to the shepherds outside Bethlehem
as they sang in grand-chorus,
"Peace on earth; goodwill to all."
    Love makes no exceptions!
Peace be with you.
    Sing!

The Black Eunuch

Yes, we eunuchs were the first openly
     transgendered.
We have a long and complex history.
     Some of us ended up in this
state voluntarily. Some had masters
that imposed such a life on us.
Those in the court knew it provided
     separation from family life,
and thus, we were trusted to be loyalists.

I served as the CFO for Candace,
     Queen of Ethiopia.
I was privileged to have had a good
education and more than my share
of perks within the queen's court.
The religions of the world, as we
     knew them, fascinated me.
I planned a trip to Jerusalem to
experience and worship in the temple.
     How a very black face in such
a place is received can be sketchy.
     It helps when you look rich.
Having royal credentials also helps.
     Certainly, I had these going for me.

     My temple plans were interrupted.
I studied on my way there. I wanted to
be prepared. I was particularly
intrigued with the prophets.
As I was reading Isaiah,
a young man happened
     out of nowhere
along the road where I had stopped.
     He came up to me with purpose
and not a hint of apprehension at

the sight of me.
"What was I reading? Did I understand it?"
    This man, Philip, spent
the next hours telling of the
    Peaceable One
who had come among them.
He was most insightful and
spoke of a simple water baptism
as a testament of their faith.

I was emboldened to ask if there
was anything to forbid my baptism.

Well, you are not part of our community.
You are a gentile, black,
    and transgendered.
You've had no formal indoctrination
    from our leadership.
How radical do you think we are?

That might have been the temple's
answer. It was not Philip's.

Of course you can be baptized!
Gentiles are in. Blacks are in.
    Eunuchs are in.
We don't maintain an out list.
    Welcome!
Let's go to the river!
    And so, we did.

There are those who maintain
lists for those who belong and those who do not.
It would seem the Peaceable One
    has no such lists.
    We all belong.

I, Paul

I'd like to go on record.
Whoever put my name on the
letters to Timothy did so for
    their own purposes.
I do not endorse their views.

I did, after all, say that there shall no
longer be male or female, and I
was known in my life to work closely
with a number of women whom I
would consider every bit as much
a part of apostolic succession
    as any man.

And apostolic succession, in my
mind, has everything to do with grace
    in discipleship
and nothing to do with bishops
    legitimizing each other.

I was pretty informal in most matters
of the community. I did hold a few
strong values, that is, to be loving, patient,
kind—you know the list.

    Being among the orthodox earlier
in my life had left me pretty scarred.
I had bought into their rigidity, even
to the point of approvingly killing
    anyone who might be a threat.
That was before being struck by Love.

While I might occasionally be coaxed
into pondering right belief or mercy,
after the scales fell from my eyes,

mercy would, in all ways, prevail.

Some of the other boys thought
I was a bit too inclusive. But even they
budged on some things regarding
ritual practices. I don't know why
they think they had to draw straws
    to replace Judas.
Twelve was no magic number when
the charge was to go make disciples.
    As far as their confined notion goes,
they would have been better off appointing
    the Marys who had proven,
beyond a doubt, their fidelity.
I never knew these women personally.
    But I did know
    they walked the walk!

    My vocation was to the gentiles.
My wise counsel on staying single
(as I was) to free one for service, it seems
to me, remains good advice.
    That it was used to enforce
celibacy as a requirement and not a
charism is most unfortunate.
    I wasn't a prude.
    If you are passionate,
be passionate. If you can forgo
sexual passions for service, then
wonderful—serve wholeheartedly.
You won't find me in the shadows
    trying to shame
human sexuality, and neither should you.

Such decisions were never meant
to be imposed by group-think or the
male hierarchy of the letter to Timothy.

(What does a bishop know of
   another's heart?)

Whatever you think of me, I'd say this:
I don't much care these days who you sleep with.
My one rant on temple orgies has been used
      to cast the condemning net
      far too widely.
I was calling out the blatant evil
that was passing for the status quo.
      It comes down to this:
Are your fruits evil or of the Spirit?

The evil fruit is covetousness, malice,
consuming envy, murder, strife, deceit, craftiness,
      gossiping, slandering, hating, insolence,
haughtiness, boastfulness—shall I go on?

While the Spirit bestows love, joy, peace,
      forbearance, kindness, goodness,
faithfulness, gentleness, and self-control.

I've said it before, and I'll say it again.
      Against such things there is no law!
What part of this do you not get?
Stop using me to condemn others.
      Stop using me to keep women
silent and subservient.

Those are your hang-ups.
      Not mine.

And to whoever wrote those instructions
on church management to Timothy,
I really wish you'd have taken credit.
      Once the scales fell,
I was far more egalitarian than

you represented in my name.

The fruits of deceit and craftiness.

Not good.

The Fisherman

Some people have no fear.
They put it out there,
    whatever it is,
    whatever the consequences.
I, among others, followed such
a man and knew well of his cousin,
    the radical baptizer.

Then there are those who speak
out often enough, but, as they say,
    "Open mouth, insert foot."
I fall in this second category.
    My tongue is directly wired
to my emotions, and what comes
out is often as big a surprise to
    me as it is to others.

I was forever doing this with our
    itinerant rabbi.
Sometimes, it would prompt
enthusiastic praise.
    "You are the rock.
I shall build my church on this rock!"
Other times, it would be
"Get behind me, Satan."

Mostly, it was a somewhat
    pitiful look,
    a shake of the head, and
the general question as to how
I and the others could be so dense.

The intellectual class within the
temple leadership was far more
obtuse and dense than we,

so, for whatever it's worth,
our denseness had nothing to do
with our lack of education.
     Wisdom is often found
among the most common.
And sometimes, it is notably absent among
     the clever and credentialed.

When the Holy Dove moves, it moves
powerfully. I was persuaded that the Spirit
could fill women and slaves.
     Well, I had seen it with my own eyes.
And I was equally persuaded in time that the
Holy Dove would fill the gentiles among us.

When Saul of Tarsus seemed to do a
     one-eighty,
there was some pressure to reject him.
I recalled the words of the rabbi:
     "If they are not against us,
     they are for us."

While I was the first to see the
     inclusivity of the Spirit for gentiles,
it would be Saul, now Paul, who would
travel great lengths to reach out to them.

Paul and I shared an egalitarian,
     socialist ethos.
Me to the point of insisting on
     a common purse.

(See the account of Ananias and Sapphira
regarding policy implementation.)

It must be said that administration of
this common purse required a lot

of oversight.
Paul, as was often the case, was
more lax on specific policies. He
seemed to go with the flow, according
to individual, congregational polity.
I was more centrist in my approach.
        He, decidedly less so.

As to the makeup of the community,
Paul, Philip, and I had no disagreements.
Women were in. Gentiles were in.
        Blacks were in. Eunuchs were in.
        Slaves were in.
We really didn't have a list for who was out,
        except those who put themselves there.

Some Jews among the group insisted on
Jewish male rights of initiation for the
gentiles. We gathered as leaders
to address this and spoke with one voice to
        put the kibosh on it.
It was easy enough to remind people
that orthodox legalism never worked.
        Why stifle the ever-more-diverse
        flock?

Like so many who followed, I am
        not sure I achieved
        the mystical level of Paul
or the abundant Spirit of the Peaceable One
        who called me from the nets.
I did have the Grace of that hard-wired,
tongue-waxing eloquence when the
        Holy Dove was pouring on me.

        Whatever my shortcomings,
it was never my intent for my teachings

to be used as a club on others.
I thought I was clear as an
    advocate for inclusion.
Later writings would take liberties,
pinning their opinions to me.

They would write in my name
    as they had for Paul.
(The bishops-boys' club needed validation
    they could never muster
from the Good News we proclaimed.)
    Oh, to be sure, they would weave in
some good poetry—inspirational, noble verse.
But then they couldn't resist.
Prop up the empire-economic system.
    Stifle women. Make it a man's world.
    Make it a game of
who is in and who is out.

(You will note they were quick to drop
my common purse policies.)

A lot of bad precedents might have
been avoided had readers pondered
the contradictions of our
    inclusive communities
to their rigidity and exclusion.
    Control freaks thrive on rigidity.

    But it is what it is. It is yours
to discern between the Good News
and patriarchal authority claims.

Of my life and its work, it can
be said that I had overcome
    the shame of denial
and would give my life rather than

ever deny a fourth time.
And I would offer peace to all.

The Martyr

My prominence in the community
    was short-lived.
I had been selected, along with six
others, to help with the administration
of the common purse and
    all that it entails.

The theory was that this would allow
the leadership to spend more time
in prayer and meditation,
    attending to the spiritual needs
while we attended to the material.
    Boundaries between the spiritual
and material were not something
I could wrap my mind around.

    I had been fairly outspoken, and
if they wanted to reign in my forthright
approach, they failed to address it with
    my new role.

Some who tolerate you when
you are in no particular
    role of authority
can find offense soon enough when you move
    "beyond your place."
They can rarely resist trying to undermine you
from the earliest opportunity. This certainly
    proved to be the case with me.

It wasn't long before tongues were wagging.
When in doubt, throw out
    wild accusations of heresy.
Question loyalties. Point the
    finger of blasphemy.

And so there I found myself standing
     before the council.
We saw our work as part of the
community, not as a departure from it.
Thus, we spoke freely and dangerously
in and around the synagogues and the temple.
     A risky formula!

No angelic face was going to assuage
their inquiry into possible
insolence of their authority.

The high priest posed the question to me:
     "Are these things so?"

I believed in the Peaceable One.
Just as he had stood for
     love above vain power,
I set off on a discourse of the
hard hearts of our history and
their refusal to heed the prophetic
     truths of our poets.

I ended leaving no doubt where
I saw their alignment in relation to
     love and vain power.

     My angelic face was crushed
with stones that day, but, just as the
Peaceable One had done at
     his crucifixion,
I would forgive my killers
as they stole the life from my body.
     My spirit was free,
while another ponderous weight
     was forged to theirs
     by their own choice.

The Brother

As an extended family, we weren't always
the most supportive of Mary and Joseph's
    firstborn.
When he first left carpentry to start his
true vocation, he caused quite a stir in
    the local synagogue as to how he saw
his life in conjunction with the Isaiah Scroll.
Of course, our extended family was a good
chunk of the group, and most were ready
    to hurl him off the brow of the hill
for blasphemy. Blasphemy may be hard
to define, but most seem to think they
    know it when they see it.
Another time, when I was with mother
and some of my siblings, we sent one of his regular
followers in to tell him we were outside and
wanted to see him. I can believe he would
have ignored us siblings, but with Mother along,
    I was shocked!
The answer came back: "Who is my mother
and who are brother and sisters?" The youngest
    spoke out, "Well, la-dee-da!"

In retrospect, I don't know why we thought
he should step out from his teaching just to
see us. We could see him anytime. He was
    right to attend to the sheep
he was feeding.

I would seek to testify to his life's work,
though I would never use my status
as his brother to try to gain influence.
    As he had taught servanthood,
so I would consider myself a
    servant of the Gospel.

My letter, though written to the Jewish
community of which we were a part,
was a testimony to the peaceable message
    my brother, the Peaceable One,
had proclaimed. He would ask,
    "Why do you call me lord
but not do what I tell you?"
    Exactly!
This notion that you could somehow
just talk about faith without living it
    hit him wrong, and me as well.

You might look at my letter as a
commentary on his poetic
    teaching to those gathered on the hill.
(The Sermon on the Mount, if you are wondering).

There are many parallels to this teaching,
and I hope no contradictions. None were
intended.

Some would contend that somehow, Paul
and I were in contradiction on doctrine.
    Nonsense!
To think I was all about works and he about
grace, only tells me, they have not pondered
the hard work we did to ensure others
knew of the magnitude of grace that is
    there for the asking.
And the humility (a grace in itself) that I tried
to convey in my own writings that saw as a core
principle of my brother's aforementioned
teaching. I did not attempt to be clever
or inventive. I am not a poet. I am one
who simply bears witness to the teachings.
    My religious notions were pretty simple:
to care for orphans and widows in their distress,

and to keep oneself unstained by the world—
    that is, free from empire's lies.
    As for my letter, may it be instructive for any
who want a narrative view of my own
    pondering of the Gospel.
Paul and I are men of faith and not lords of
doctrine. Ponder, pray, and act.

    I, James, remain a dear brother,
your faithful servant!

The Loved One

People are eager to be literalists
until it doesn't fit well with their
narrative of what can and can't
be normative to their worldview.

Bonds of affection are not restricted
    to those of the opposite sex.

King David's first wife, the daughter
of Saul, despised him. She had good
reason. Then, he made Bathsheba his wife
    by murder and by force.
She would connive to make her son,
sired by the king, king.
    Not much of a love story there,
despite our continued admiration of
    the famous king.

Wives aside, the only person David
seemed to love throughout his life
and until the loved one's death
    was Johnathon.

Alexander would reign over Macedonia,
Egypt, and Asia, and muddle through
marriages not much differently from
David. He would keep at his side his
loyal comrade Hephaestion and
morn him greatly when he died.
(Alexander's own life would end
    soon thereafter.)

The Peaceable One was not married, and
    while others in our band would
scatter like a frightened flock of quail,

I alone of the twelve would be there with his mother
on the day of his execution.

I loved him. He loved me.
He looked down at his mother
and said, "Behold, your son."
He looked and me and said,
"Behold, your mother."

Make of that what you will.

The Poet of Patmos

Having a common name like John
can cause confusion easy enough.
Too many people will say,
   "Well, John said..."
I, John, the Poet of Patmos, had lots
to say. I hope you'll not assign any
consternation with my writings to
other Johns innocent of my
   tangled, metaphoric thoughts.
I'm not worried about some other
John taking credit for my work.
I just don't want to implicate others
in views that I have set forward.

Having that out of the way lets me
get to my real concern. Yes, I
believe mightily in the inspiration
   of the Holy Dove. I even believe
much of the writing I did came from
   powers and inspirations well
beyond the human limits of my mind.
   Words are art for me.
I find their composition to be
a remarkably instructive process.
   I awaken some mornings
with such rich images and specific phrases
in my mind that I must sit down
and honor what flows from that
   unknown place.

Here is the thing you need to know
about good poetry: It enables
   a search for truth.
It may not be factual. It may portend
to things that will happen, or it may not.

That is not the point.
    To take a poet's work,
inspired as it is (or may be) by the Holy Dove,
and make it a one-time fit for your
agenda has missed the very point of
the poetry. I'll say it again.
    Good poetry enables
    a search for truth.
It is not a historical account
or a future foretelling, though
you will find it in history, and you
can trust it to speak to future
    generations as well.

(Read the poet Amos, and you'll see
what I mean.)

    I suppose I did get a little carried away.
The imagery just filled my imagination.
To boil down the truth of my telling is this:
    The struggles of evil against good
can seem unending. It seems to me,
    man is on a course of self-
destruction using powers that
will increase in magnitude and awe
    as we march on through history.
I tried to say poetically how crazy
it could become. There is always
    enough war
to make the unimaginable imaginable.
    It is all too easy for
the churches to be complicit
in the warring madness and evil
    deeds that abound.
I may have dealt too much on war
imagery, but it is, sadly, what people
    relate to in our time.

Most poets bring themselves
out of the darkness and back
    to the light. I did. "There
shall be a new heaven and a new
earth" sums up my hope for peace.
    This must be the hope
and the work of every generation.
    It is not for the faint-hearted.

    Oh, and one other thing:
Someone else added that last line.
I'm not concerned about
    intellectual property rights
to my apocalyptic collection
or what others make of the writing.
Some scribe, perhaps, decided their canon
    needed some finality
as though the Holy Dove's
dictation was finished.
    As long as Creation groans,
so shall the Holy Dove breathe
her poetic voice through her poets.
    Never quit listening!

An Afterword

The Creators

As the atom consists of three parts,
    so you might think of
the force of Love, which brought
forth all that is. You may choose
to hold to purely rational views
of happenstance and natural selection,
    in which case you may
think of us as protons, electrons, and
neutrons, primary building blocks.
    The seemingly infinite
nature of the universe ought to
    humble the greatest minds.
Great minds are typically humble.
That some think of this loving force
as the father and mother of their being
is logical enough. Creation is the
ultimate bible, or whatever you wish
to call your holy book. If what you
    observe of the cosmos
is contradicted by your own held
beliefs, then it is time to
    dig for humility.
The cosmos is not wrong. You are.

Many of our children have sensed
a Great Spirit who breathes life to them
and breathes our Words to them. We
are noun, verb, and adjective. We
    are energy, mass, and light.
We are complexity, depth, and unity.
We are love, logos, and liberation.
We are a great pillar of fire. We are the

mighty wind blowing where it will.
     We are the still small voice.
Some have attempted to make us
a very human-like form. We are not
offended. We understand how
     incomprehensible this all is.
Call us God or Yahweh or Allah
     or "Hey, y'all."
We're not picky about names.
Just know, we are far more than
     the male authority figure
you have used to make others subservient.
Gender is a procreative necessity. It is
not essential to atoms, quarks,
     fractals, dark energy,
suns, moons, stars, or gravity, yet
we are in all these things.
We should not be invoked for your
     own lust of power.
We should not be proclaimed in
     certitudes, even by poets.
We are beyond words, beyond images,
     beyond imaginations.

What is a day? If we are the
     god of the Milky Way,
than perhaps it is two hundred
million years, as planet Earth
     would define a day.
For that is the time it takes for
one revolution of this galaxy.
     But we are more than
the god of the Milky Way. Our eternal
nature is patient as well as loving,
and if things take a few billion
years, we are in no hurry.
     We are beyond time.

Beyond the constraints of even
     the richest metaphor.
Beyond intricate argument, scientific
formula, and doctrinal formulation.

     You earthlings have the most
remarkable gift. Try to imagine
anything better. As far as your eye can see
and your telescope can reach, there is no better.
     The awesome beauty
and gift of love you are endowed with
in this home, your blue celestial orb,
ought to be enough to inspire great lives of
     unceasing gratitude.
It ought to instill great care and
     continuous marvel.

     If you can't see it now,
will you ever? Stop trying to
get to heaven. Recognize heaven now.
     You are in the nightmare of
greed and destruction.
     Awaken!
Creation has dawned, and
     you are missing it!

Made in the USA
Coppell, TX
19 July 2020